Service

Life Together Resources

Building Character Together series

Authenticity: Living a Spiritually Healthy Life

Friendship: Living a Connected Life

Faith: Living a Transformed Life

Service: Living a Meaningful Life

Influence: Living a Contagious Life

Obedience: Living a Yielded Life

Doing Life Together series

Beginning Life Together

Connecting with God's Family

Growing to Be Like Christ

Developing Your SHAPE to Serve Others

Sharing Your Life Mission Every Day

Surrendering Your Life to God's Pleasure

Experiencing Christ Together series

Beginning in Christ Together

Connecting in Christ Together

Growing in Christ Together

Serving Like Christ Together

Sharing Christ Together

Surrendering to Christ Together

SERVICE

living a *Meaningful* life

BRETT and DEE EASTMAN
TODD and DENISE WENDORFF

ZONDERVAN.com/
AUTHORTRACKER
follow your favorite authors

We want to hear from you. Please send your comments about this book to us in care of zreview@zondervan.com. Thank you.

Service
Copyright © 2007 by Brett and Deanna Eastman, Todd and Denise Wendorff

Requests for information should be addressed to:

Zondervan, *Grand Rapids, Michigan 49530*

ISBN-10: 0-310-24993-7
ISBN-13: 978-0-310-24993-1

Interior design by Melissa Elenbaas

Printed in the United States of America

07 08 09 10 11 12 13 • 10 9 8 7 6 5 4 3 2 1

Contents

ACKNOWLEDGMENTS

It's been quite a ride ever since our first series was published back in 2002. Literally thousands of churches and small groups have studied the LIFE TOGETHER series to the tune of over two million copies sold. As we said back in our first series, "By the grace of God and a clear call on the hearts of a few, our dream has become a reality." Now, our dream has entered the realm of being beyond all that we could ask or imagine.

To see thousands and thousands of people step out to gather a few friends and do a Bible study with an easy-to-use DVD curriculum has been amazing. People have grown in their faith, introduced their friends to Christ, and found deeper connection with God. Thanks to God for planting this idea in our hearts. Thanks to all of those who took a risk by stepping out to lead a group for six weeks for the very first time. This has been truly amazing.

Once again, a great team was instrumental to creating this new series in community. From the start back at Saddleback with Todd and Denise Wendorff and Brett and Dee Eastman, the writing team has grown. Special thanks to John Fischer, yes, THE John Fischer, for writing all of the introductions to these studies. Also, thanks to our LIFE TOGETHER writing team: Pam Marotta, Peggy Matthews Rose, and Teri Haymaker. Last, but not least, thanks to Allen White for keeping this project on track and getting the ball in the net.

Thank you to our church families who have loved and supported us and helped us grow over the years. There are so many pastors, staff, and members that have taught us so much. We love you all.

Finally, thank you to our beloved families who have lived with us, laughed at us, and loved us through it all. We love doing our lives together with you.

OUTLINE OF EACH SESSION

Most people want to live a healthy, balanced spiritual life, but few achieve this by themselves. And most small groups struggle to balance all of God's purposes in their meetings. Groups tend to overemphasize one of the five purposes, perhaps fellowship or discipleship. Rarely is there a healthy balance that includes evangelism, ministry, and worship. That's why we've included all of these elements in this study so you can live a healthy, balanced spiritual life over time.

A typical group session will include the following:

CONNECTING WITH GOD'S FAMILY (FELLOWSHIP). The foundation for spiritual growth is an intimate connection with God and his family. A few people who really know you and who earn your trust provide a place to experience the life Jesus invites you to live. This section of each session typically offers you two options: You can get to know your whole group by using the icebreaker question, or you can check in with one or two group members — your spiritual partner(s) — for a deeper connection and encouragement in your spiritual journey.

GROWING TO BE LIKE CHRIST (DISCIPLESHIP). Here is where you come face-to-face with Scripture. In core passages you'll explore what the Bible teaches about character through the lives of God's people in Scripture. The focus won't be on accumulating information but on how we should live in light of the Word of God. We want to help you apply the Scriptures practically, creatively, and from your heart as well as your head. At the end of the day, allowing the timeless truths from God's Word to transform our lives in Christ is our greatest aim.

FOR DEEPER STUDY. If you want to dig deeper into more Bible passages about the topic at hand, we've provided additional passages and questions. Your group may choose to do study homework ahead of each meeting in order to cover more biblical material. Or you as an individual may choose to study the For Deeper Study passages on your own. If you prefer not to do study homework, the Growing section will

provide you with plenty to discuss within the group. These options allow individuals or the whole group to go deeper in their study, while still accommodating those who can't do homework.

You can record your discoveries in your journal. We encourage you to read some of your insights to a friend (spiritual partner) for accountability and support. Spiritual partners may check in each week over the phone, through email, or at the beginning of the group meeting.

DEVELOPING YOUR GIFTS TO SERVE OTHERS (MINISTRY). Jesus trained his disciples to discover and develop their gifts to serve others. God has designed you uniquely to serve him in a way no other person can. This section will help you discover and use your God-given design. It will also encourage your group to discover your unique design as a community. In this study, you'll put into practice what you've learned in the Bible study by taking a step to serve others. These simple steps will take your group on a faith journey that could change your lives forever.

SHARING YOUR LIFE MISSION EVERY DAY (EVANGELISM). Many people skip over this aspect of the Christian life because it's scary, relationally awkward, or simply too much work for their busy schedules. But Jesus wanted all of his disciples to help outsiders connect with him, to know him personally. This doesn't mean preaching on street corners. It could mean welcoming a few newcomers into your group, hosting a short-term group in your home, or walking through this study with a friend. In this study, you'll have an opportunity to go beyond Bible study to biblical living.

SURRENDERING YOUR LIFE FOR GOD'S PLEASURE (WORSHIP). God is most pleased by a heart that is fully his. Each group session will give you a chance to surrender your heart to God in prayer and worship. You may read a psalm together, share a page in your journal, or sing a song to close your meeting. (A LIFE TOGETHER Worship DVD/CD series, produced by Maranatha!, is available through www.lifetogether. com.) If you have never prayed aloud in a group before, no one will put pressure on you. Instead, you'll experience the support of others who are praying for you. This time will knit your hearts in community and help you surrender your hurts and dreams into the hands of the One who knows you best.

STUDY NOTES. This section provides background notes on the Bible passage(s) you examine in the Growing section. You may want to refer to these notes during your group meeting or as a reference for those doing additional study.

REFLECTIONS. Each week on the Reflections pages we provide Scriptures to read and reflect on between group meetings. We suggest you use this section to seek God at home throughout the week. This time at home should begin and end with prayer. Don't get in a hurry; take enough time to hear God's direction.

SUBGROUPS FOR DISCUSSION AND PRAYER. In some of the sessions of this series we have suggested you separate into groups of two to four for discussion or prayer. This is to assure greater participation and deeper discussion.

What are you going to do when summer is over?" he asked. He and I had shared duties during the first week of summer camp where I worked as a new college graduate, and I had been blown away by his rapport with high-school kids and his proven speaking gifts.

"Go to seminary," I answered.

"Why seminary?" he asked.

"Well, because I want to go into the ministry and that's what you're supposed to do, I guess."

"Not necessarily," he said, confusing me. "I just finished seminary and if you come with me, I'll teach you everything I know."

Well, I didn't have to think long about that. Here I had a man promising me what an institution was supposed to provide. And I knew his training would be right in the midst of ministry, where the action was. I went with the man and never regretted it.

This man turned out to be my most influential mentor, but not for the reasons I committed myself to him. The most important part was his humanness and vulnerability. He taught me, but he also walked with me and let me walk with him. I got to know his wife, his family, his good and bad sides, and not all of it was pretty. Looking back, I think I learned more from watching him struggle and blow it than from watching his successes. It gave me hope to see that *we* don't affect people; *God* does through us and, in some cases, in spite of us!

CONNECTING WITH GOD'S FAMILY   20 MIN.

Whether or not we have the spiritual gift of leadership, we all have the power to influence others. In fact, each of us *is* an influence — either for good or for bad. What kind of influence are you? In this session we'll talk about the influence of Moses, a man initially reluctant to lead but whose life eventually became a model of leadership abilities.

1. Talk about someone who was a powerful influence in your life. How did that person inspire you?

2. We recommend that you rotate host homes on a regular basis and let the hosts lead the meeting. We've come to realize that healthy groups rotate leadership. This helps to develop every member's ability to shepherd a few people in a safe environment. Even Jesus gave others the opportunity to serve alongside him (Mark 6:30–44). People need opportunities to experiment with ways in which God may have gifted them. Your group will give you all the encouragement you need before, during, and after the session. Some groups like to let the host lead the meeting each week, while others like to let one person host while another person leads.

   The Small Group Calendar on page 91 is a tool for planning who will host and lead each meeting and who will provide refreshments. Take a few minutes to plan for your next five meetings. Don't pass this up! It will greatly impact your group.

3. With any group, whether you are just forming or have been together for a while, it's good to review and consider your shared values from time to time. You'll find a Small Group Agreement on pages 89–90 delineating those values we have found to be the most useful in building and sustaining healthy, balanced groups. If your group is new, you may also find helpful the Frequently Asked Questions on pages 86–88.

GROWING TO BE LIKE CHRIST   40 MIN.

Typically when we think of Moses, we get mental images of a man who looked a lot like Charlton Heston holding up stone tablets or parting the Red Sea. We think of him as a dynamic, forceful leader—and he was! But his place in history did not come about because it is what he wanted to be when he grew up.

When God spoke to him from the burning bush, Moses' first reaction was, "O God—you've got the wrong guy! You can't mean me. I can't convince Pharaoh to let your people go. Besides, I stutter!" Only someone as powerful as God could hear him over the sound of his knocking knees. Moses knew there was no way he could do this—and on his own, he couldn't. What he didn't realize at that moment was that he would not be going alone. God would be his partner. God, who had called him, would give him what he needed to do the job.

But Moses' faith needed some nudging. He could not get past his personal insecurities. "Please, Lord," he begged, "send *anyone* but me!" God reminded him who was in charge: this mission was not about Moses' weakness, but God's plan and God's power. Still, Moses protested his fitness to serve.

Like the father of a disobedient teenager, God was decidedly less than pleased with Moses at this moment. He loved Moses and knew the plans he had for him; he also knew they rested in Moses' willingness to surrender his will for God's. Because Moses was being so stubborn, God agreed to let Moses' brother Aaron do the talking. "I'll tell you what to say," God directed, "and you'll tell Aaron what to say." And Moses became the original "middle man"!

Truthfully, we can't fault Moses too much for being reluctant. Besides the fear of public speaking most of us have inherited, there were plenty of reasons not to go on this risky mission. But in the end and after a fashion, he obeyed. Moses found his adequacy in God.

Read Exodus 3:11–12; 4:10–17:

> But Moses said to God, "Who am I, that I should go to Pharaoh and bring the Israelites out of Egypt?" [12]And God said, "I will be with you. And this will be the sign to you that it is I who have sent you: When you have brought the people out of Egypt, you will worship God on this mountain."
>
> 4:10Moses said to the LORD, "O Lord, I have never been eloquent, neither in the past nor since you have spoken to your servant. I am slow of speech and tongue." [11]The LORD said to him, "Who gave man his mouth? Who makes him deaf or mute? Who gives him sight or makes him blind? Is it not I, the LORD? [12]Now go; I will help you speak and will teach you what to say." [13]But Moses said, "O Lord, please send someone else to do it." [14]Then the LORD's anger burned against Moses and he said, "What about your brother, Aaron the Levite? I know he can speak well. He is already on his way to meet you, and his heart will be glad when he sees you. [15]You shall speak to him and put words in his mouth; I will help both of you speak and will teach you what to do. [16]He will

speak to the people for you, and it will be as if he were your mouth and as if you were God to him. ¹⁷But take this staff in your hand so you can perform miraculous signs with it."

4. In Exodus 3:11, Moses began, "Who am I, that I should go ...?" Do you think most people would consider this reluctance or modesty? Explain your answer.

5. Why did Moses think he was wrong for this role?

6. How do our natural abilities generally influence our ministry decisions?

7. What did God want Moses to understand (see Exodus 3:12a)?

8. Read Exodus 4:10. What was Moses struggling to get past?

9. How would you advise a fellow believer who confessed feelings of inadequacy regarding a job or task they were being called on to perform?

10. God persisted in his attempt to make Moses see the issue from his perspective (see Exodus 4:11 – 12). How would memorizing this passage help you next time you are called upon to speak up for God?

11. In Exodus 4:15 – 16, God instructed Moses to appoint Aaron as his spokesman, telling Aaron what to say on God's behalf. Consider the trust God placed in Moses to do that. Even though you are not Moses, what does this scene say to you about how we are to represent God before others?

12. As he set out to obey God's commands, Moses was comforted by God's promise as represented in his shepherd's staff (Exodus 4:17). What can you rely on in a similar way to remind you of God's constant presence and power?

FOR DEEPER STUDY

Read Acts 6:1 – 7:

In those days when the number of disciples was increasing, the Grecian Jews among them complained against the Hebraic Jews because their widows were being overlooked in the daily distribution of food. [2]So the Twelve gathered all the disciples together and said, "It would not be right for us to neglect the ministry of the word of God in order to wait on tables. [3]Brothers, choose seven men from among you who are known to be full of the Spirit and wisdom. We will turn this responsibility over to them [4]and will give our attention to prayer and the ministry of the word." [5]This proposal pleased the whole group. They chose Stephen, a man full of faith and of the Holy Spirit; also Philip, Procorus, Nicanor, Timon, Parmenas, and Nicolas from Antioch, a convert to Judaism. [6]They presented these men to the apostles, who prayed and laid their hands on them. [7]So the word of God spread. The number of disciples in Jerusalem increased rapidly, and a large number of priests became obedient to the faith.

This passage recounts the time the twelve apostles delegated seven others to wait tables and serve the widows among the young household of Christ. They did this out of a need to keep peace in the family, while at the same time not neglecting the critical roles of prayer and ministry of the Word. The needs in all churches increase as the church grows.

Whether or not you are in a position of leadership in your church or group, how can following the model of these original apostles help resolve problems you observe or become aware of?

DEVELOPING YOUR GIFTS TO SERVE OTHERS   10 MIN.

13. God offers us his resources and power to do whatever he calls us to, just as he did for Moses. When God asks you to do something you don't think you can do, how can you learn to trust that he will give you what you need to do the job?

14. One habit that helps to strengthen our resolve to do God's will is to connect with someone about the things God speaks into our hearts and the areas where he challenges us to grow.

Pair up with someone in your group (we suggest that men partner with men and women with women) to be your "spiritual partner" during this study. He or she doesn't have to be your best friend but will simply encourage you to complete the goals you set for yourself throughout this study. Following through on a resolution is tough when you're on your own, but we've found it makes all the difference to have a partner cheering us on.

On pages 92–93 is a Personal Health Plan, a chart for keeping track of your spiritual progress. In the box that says "WHO are you connecting with spiritually?" write your partner's name. You can see that the health plan contains space for you to record the ups and downs of your progress each week in the column labeled "My Progress." And now with your spiritual partner you don't have to do it alone, but together with a friend.

For now, don't worry about the WHAT, WHERE, WHEN, and HOW questions on the health plan.

SHARING YOUR LIFE MISSION EVERY DAY   10 MIN.

15. Have feelings of inadequacy held you back from sharing God's message of love and hope with others? Why not invite someone to join your small group next week, and see what God does? In order to identify those around you who might benefit from this study, we have provided the Circles of Life diagram below. This tool can help you think about the people you come in contact with on a regular basis. Take a minute or two now to write down the names of those you know who might benefit from a small group. Then, commit to inviting them next week. Even if your invitation is not accepted, God is pleased by your obedience.

CIRCLES OF LIFE

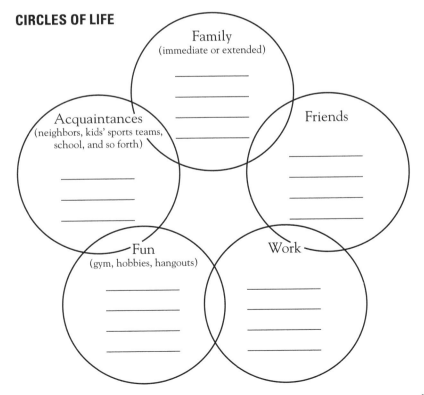

16. While you are working through the rest of this session, pass around a sheet of paper or one of you pass your study guide opened to the Small Group Roster on pages 125–126. Have everyone write down their contact information, then ask someone to make copies or type up a list with everyone's information and email it to the group this week.

SURRENDERING YOUR LIFE FOR GOD'S PLEASURE   15–20 MIN.

17. Share your prayer requests with the group. Then close your time together by praying not only for these requests but for each other as you seek to overcome any hang-ups that might be keeping you from the role God has for you. Remember, God's power is available to meet your needs. Write down group members' prayer requests on the Prayer and Praise Report page provided on page 22. As God answers these requests, be sure to celebrate how he is working among and through your group.

18. Note the Reflections pages at the end of this session. Use these in your quiet time this week. There are five daily Scripture readings from the study and a place to record your summary of the five reflections on day six.

STUDY NOTES

Pharaoh. Pharaoh is a title used to refer to the monarchs of ancient Egypt that ruled during the pre-Christian, pre-Islamic period.

And bring the Israelites out of Egypt. It all started well with the children of Israel when Joseph, the eleventh son of Jacob, whom his brothers sold into slavery, became second only to the ruling pharaoh. Under that pharaoh's blessing, Joseph brought his whole family to live in Egypt due to a famine in Canaan. But subsequent pharaohs were not as kind to Jacob's descendants. As the Israelites grew in numbers, the Egyptians forced them into slavery to keep them from gaining power. They had suffered over four hundred years of slavery when Moses came along (see Exodus 12:40).

The LORD's anger burned against Moses. Sometimes it is hard for us to understand why God is presented this way in the Bible. He appears to be a God who changes his mind, who can be bargained with—even cajoled—

and who expresses a wide spectrum of human emotions including anger, impatience, and even revenge. Keep in mind, however, that this is how these emotions *appear to us*, tainted as we are by sin. From God's point of view, his thoughts and motives are always pure, but we are not able to always see from his perspective. Seeing God through our human eyes is going to always be limited; but that is still the only way we can describe him.

Aaron the Levite. Levites were descendants of the tribe of Levi who were set apart as priestly servants to dismantle, carry, and erect the tabernacle as well as to serve the needs of the fellow priests (see Numbers 1:47–54).

PRAYER AND PRAISE REPORT

Briefly share your prayer requests with the large group, making notations below. Then gather in small groups of two to four to pray for each other.

Date: _____

PRAYER REQUESTS

_____

_____

_____

_____

_____

_____

_____

_____

_____

_____

_____

_____

PRAISE REPORT

_____

_____

_____

_____

_____

_____

_____

_____

REFLECTIONS

Each day read the daily verse(s) and give prayerful consideration to what you learn about God, his Spirit, and his place in your life. Then record your thoughts, insights, or prayer in the Reflect section. On day six record a summary of what you have learned over the entire week through this study.

DAY 1   *"The LORD said to him, 'Who gave man his mouth? Who makes him deaf or mute? Who gives him sight or makes him blind? Is it not I, the LORD? Now go; I will help you speak and will teach you what to say.'" (Exodus 4:11 – 12)*

REFLECT: _____

_____

_____

_____

_____

_____

_____

_____

DAY 2   *"Trust in the LORD with all your heart; do not depend on your own understanding. Seek his will in all you do, and he will direct your paths. Don't be impressed with your own wisdom. Instead, fear the LORD and turn your back on evil." (Proverbs 3:5 – 7 NLT)*

REFLECT: _____

_____

_____

_____

_____

_____

_____

DAY 3   *"On my account you will be brought before governors and kings as witnesses to them and to the Gentiles. But when they arrest you, do not worry about what to say or how to say it. At that time you will be given what to say, for it will not be you speaking, but the Spirit of your Father speaking through you." (Matthew 10:18–20)*

REFLECT: _____

_____

_____

_____

_____

_____

_____

_____

_____

_____

DAY 4   *"You are the light of the world. A city on a hill cannot be hidden. Neither do people light a lamp and put it under a bowl. Instead they put it on its stand, and it gives light to everyone in the house. In the same way, let your light shine before men, that they may see your good deeds and praise your Father in heaven." (Matthew 5:14–16)*

REFLECT: _____

_____

_____

_____

_____

_____

_____

_____

_____

_____

DAY 5   *"I urge you, as aliens and strangers in the world, to abstain from sinful desires, which war against your soul. Live such good lives among the pagans that, though they accuse you of doing wrong, they may see your good deeds and glorify God on the day he visits us." (1 Peter 2:11–12)*

REFLECT: _____

_____

_____

_____

_____

_____

_____

_____

_____

_____

_____

_____

DAY 6   Use the following space to write any thoughts God has put in your heart and mind about the things discussed during session one and/or during your Reflections time this week.

SUMMARY: _____

_____

_____

_____

_____

_____

_____

_____

_____

_____

_____

_____

_____

GOD-DIRECTED SERVICE — DEBORAH AND DORCAS

'll always remember my mother's memorial service. It was held at the church where she spent the last half century of her life. The surprise was when people were asked to share how her life had affected them. There was a steady stream of people, many of whom I knew nothing about, coming forward to testify to my mother's role in their spiritual formation. And they all had primarily the same thing to say — how they were encouraged by my mother, her counsel to them, and mostly her prayers for them. She had a corkboard in her closet where she knelt and prayed for hours at a time. We counted 417 people tacked to that corkboard whom she was praying for regularly when she died. The prevailing question was how many people it was going to take to replace her in God's kingdom on earth.

I have a feeling we're going to find out about large numbers of people like this in heaven who faithfully and quietly served many people during their lives with hardly any recognition. No matter. That's not why they did it. If their own recognition had been their motivation, as Jesus said, they would have already received their reward. Part of laying up treasures for ourselves in heaven is being willing to be silent servants. These are the ones God will have special recognition for in heaven, and a crown awaiting.

CONNECTING WITH GOD'S FAMILY   20 MIN.

Using your talents for God may involve stepping out in the spotlight, or it may require your quiet, steady presence in a background role. Whatever we are cast to do, it's important to realize we are all "extras" in God's movie. He is the only star.

Deborah and Dorcas lived centuries apart and performed dramatically different roles, but their hearts for God were in one place. In this session, we'll examine using our abilities to serve God, however he requires them.

1. As a kid, were you ever in a school play? Share your experience. Were you the star, costar, or the stage manager?

2. On pages 96–97 of this study guide you'll find the Personal Health Assessment. Take a few minutes right now to rate yourself in each area. You won't have to share your scores with the group.

- What's one area that is going well and one area that's not going as well? Don't be embarrassed; everybody struggles in one area or another.

- Take another moment and write in a simple step (or goal) under the "WHAT is your next step for growth?" question on the Personal Health Plan on page 92.

3. Pair up with your spiritual partner and discuss what type of role you always hope to get when you think about serving at work, at church, or in your group. Has the Personal Health Assessment changed your thinking? How?

GROWING TO BE LIKE CHRIST   40 MIN.

To borrow a phrase from Charles Dickens, "It was the best of times, it was the worst of times." Following the death of Joshua, Israel came under the rule of judges. For a period of about two hundred years, Israel had no central vision caster. For a while, all was well. But in time, the tribes became scattered and weak. External pressure would eventually drive them to seek a king. For now, however, God elected those whose hearts he could rely on to lead the charge — unlikely leaders, not always big, strong "macho" men — but always people who saw God's bigger picture.

As one of God's judges, Deborah was an influential woman, a respected community leader who respected others. So great was her power that Barak, Israel's military leader at that time, refused to go into battle unless Deborah accompanied him.

It's hard to know exactly what to think of Barak, but there is no doubt Deborah had a heart for God and for God's people. Riding into battle at Barak's side was not her idea, but her willingness to go when called reveals who Deborah's true leader was. She rode with Barak, but God ruled her heart.

Read Judges 4:8–10:

*Barak said to her, "If you go with me, I will go; but if you
don't go with me, I won't go." ⁹"Very well," Deborah said, "I
will go with you. But because of the way you are going about
this, the honor will not be yours, for the LORD will hand Sisera
over to a woman." So Deborah went with Barak to Kedesh,
¹⁰where he summoned Zebulun and Naphtali. Ten thousand
men followed him, and Deborah also went with him.*

No one in the Joppa Community Church could believe the
news—how could Dorcas be gone? Hadn't she just been in the
prayer meeting last week? Every one of them had at least one gar-
ment she had made, just for them, in their closet. And when she
wasn't sewing, her hands were busy doing some other needed task.
Clearly, she'd been a quiet but powerful force in their midst.

Then someone whispered it—Peter is over in Lydda, just down
the road! Word on the street was he'd been healing people there.
Maybe, if they got word to him, he could come and lay hands on her
and … well, with God, anything is possible.

How could Peter say no? The look in the two men's eyes tore at
his heart. He went with them to the upper room where she lay—
and found it filled with grieving people. He'd never seen such a
crowd! This Dorcas must have been someone very special.

After clearing the room, Peter knelt beside her bed and prayed.
And then he called her name. "Tabitha!" he said, using the name
and tone of voice her father must have used, "get up!"

Dorcas's eyelids fluttered, then opened. She smiled to see Peter
there before her, welcomed his hand as he reached for her and drew
her to her feet.

"Come, everyone!" he called from the open door at the top of
the stairs. "She is back."

And all of Joppa rejoiced.

Read Acts 9:36–42:

*In Joppa there was a disciple named Tabitha (which, when
translated, is Dorcas), who was always doing good and helping the poor. ³⁷About that time she became sick and died,
and her body was washed and placed in an upstairs room.
³⁸Lydda was near Joppa; so when the disciples heard that*

Peter was in Lydda, they sent two men to him and urged him, "Please come at once!" ³⁹Peter went with them, and when he arrived he was taken upstairs to the room. All the widows stood around him, crying and showing him the robes and other clothing that Dorcas had made while she was still with them. ⁴⁰Peter sent them all out of the room; then he got down on his knees and prayed. Turning toward the dead woman, he said, "Tabitha, get up." She opened her eyes, and seeing Peter she sat up. ⁴¹He took her by the hand and helped her to her feet. Then he called the believers and the widows and presented her to them alive. ⁴²This became known all over Joppa, and many people believed in the Lord.

4. Consider Deborah's words to Barak in Judges 4:9. What do they say to you about the importance of serving God willingly?

5. The stories of Deborah and Dorcas are completely different, yet they both point to the power of an individual life yielded to God's service. When you think of Dorcas's story, which do you think spoke louder to the people in her community — her miraculous healing or the fact that she "was always doing good and helping the poor" (verse 36)? Why?

6. How do these stories speak to you about the power of a life lived well for God, no matter what he asks you to do?

7. In what ways do Deborah and Dorcas embody God-directed service?

8. Who do you most identify with — Deborah or Dorcas (or Barak)? Why?

9. Take a moment to recall someone who stood out in your life as a servant of God. How and why did that person especially impact your life?

FOR DEEPER STUDY

In the Acts 9:36 – 42 passage, we looked at the gifts of Dorcas, a charitable seamstress who took obvious care of her community. But the passage really focuses on the gifts and abilities of Peter, the overzealous fisherman turned on-fire apostle. Look back at verses 32 – 35. What had Peter accomplished, in Jesus' name, just prior to being called to Joppa?

By the time Peter arrived in Joppa, he found that Dorcas's believing friends had prepared her body for burial, but had not yet buried her. It was customary in that culture to bury the dead before sundown. Yet they lingered in the room with Dorcas's body. What does this suggest to you about the attitude of their hearts once they heard Peter was coming?

When a person builds or acquires a reputation for a special ability, as Peter had, what care do you think they should take that their fame does not exceed their gift or distort their sense of self?

Read Judges 4:6–8. Whose command did Barak obey, albeit conditionally? Was there a consequence to Barak's conditional obedience? What was it (see verse 9)?

DEVELOPING YOUR GIFTS TO SERVE OTHERS   10 MIN.

In addition to a willingness to serve God through their giftedness, both Deborah and Dorcas shared a deep love for God's people.

10. Describe how your love for others influences how you develop and use your abilities to serve them.

11. What can you do to serve within your small group? Turn to the Gifts Inventory on pages 101–103 of the appendix. Prayerfully consider whether the biblical definition of each gift describes you. Remember, you can have more than one gift, but everyone has at least one. Allow at least ten minutes for everyone to evaluate the gifts listed. Then a few of you share one or two gifts you are certain you have. As a group, affirm each other's gifts. Note that this is not a complete list of spiritual gifts, but does contain most of the "serving gifts" identified in the New Testament.

Then turn to the Team Roles on pages 98–100. Based on the serving gifts you identified for yourself, commit to joining one of the teams listed there and taking the Crawl step to serve your group during this study.

SHARING YOUR LIFE MISSION EVERY DAY   10 MIN.

12. As a group, spend a few minutes discussing a project or ministry that together you could undertake as an outreach to your community. Brainstorm ideas now and someone volunteer to research other ideas and/or ask your pastor or other church leader about any unmet needs your group might meet. Be prepared to report the status of this planned effort during session five.

SURRENDERING YOUR LIFE FOR GOD'S PLEASURE   15–20 MIN.

13. Briefly discuss how you can make the most of praying for one another. Is there something you can do to maximize your prayer time as a group? This could mean making sure prayer doesn't get forgotten, recording requests and praises, starting a prayer chain, or sending email requests between meetings. Make praying for each other a priority, both in and outside your group meeting, and be sure to celebrate God's answers. Make a habit of recording your prayer requests on the Prayer and Praise Report (page 35 for this session).

If this lesson has spoken to you about an attitude or desire you need to release to God, ask your group to pray with you now for the courage to make the change God is revealing to your heart.

14. Use the Reflections verses at the end of this session in your quiet time this week. Record any thoughts or direction you receive from the Lord in the space provided.

STUDY NOTES

Sisera. A Canaanite general who commanded Jabin's army in the war against Deborah and Barak, and who was slain by Jael, wife of Heber, thus fulfilling the prophecy that Sisera would fall at the hands of a woman. See Judges 4:17–21.

Zebulun and Naphtali. Two of the twelve sons of Jacob. This would refer to the fighting men of those two tribes as the ones who went to war against Sisera.

There was a disciple named Tabitha. Tabitha (Dorcas) is the only woman called a "disciple" by name in the New Testament (Acts 9:36).

He took her by the hand and helped her to her feet. Peter was only fulfilling his divine commission that Jesus gave his disciples in Matthew 10:8: "Heal the sick, raise the dead, cleanse those who have leprosy, drive out demons. Freely you have received, freely give."

Peter sent them all out of the room. Peter must have adopted this behavior from watching Jesus. Jesus never made a display of his healings and often told people not to tell anyone what had happened or who had healed them.

Briefly share your prayer requests with the large group, making notations below. Then gather in small groups of two to four to pray for each other.

Date: _____

PRAYER REQUESTS

_____

_____

_____

_____

_____

_____

_____

_____

_____

_____

_____

PRAISE REPORT

_____

_____

_____

_____

_____

_____

_____

_____

REFLECTIONS

Each day read the daily verse(s) and give prayerful consideration to what you learn about God, his Spirit, and his place in your life. Then record your thoughts, insights, or prayer in the Reflect section. On day six record a summary of what you have learned over the entire week through this study.

DAY 1   *"There are different kinds of gifts, but the same Spirit. There are different kinds of service, but the same Lord. There are different kinds of working, but the same God works all of them in all men."* (1 Corinthians 12:4–6)

REFLECT: _____

_____

_____

_____

_____

_____

_____

_____

DAY 2   *"Now to each one the manifestation of the Spirit is given for the common good."* (1 Corinthians 12:7)

REFLECT: _____

_____

_____

_____

_____

_____

_____

DAY 3 *"All these are the work of one and the same Spirit, and he gives them to each one, just as he determines. The body is a unit, though it is made up of many parts; and though all its parts are many, they form one body. So it is with Christ." (1 Corinthians 12:11–12)*

REFLECT: _____

_____

_____

_____

_____

_____

_____

_____

_____

_____

_____

DAY 4 *" 'Which of these three do you think was a neighbor to the man who fell into the hands of robbers?' The expert in the law replied, 'The one who had mercy on him.' Jesus told him, 'Go and do likewise.' " (Luke 10:36–37)*

REFLECT: _____

_____

_____

_____

_____

_____

_____

_____

_____

_____

_____

DAY 5   *"Give to everyone who asks you, and if anyone takes what belongs to you, do not demand it back. Do to others as you would have them do to you. If you love those who love you, what credit is that to you? Even 'sinners' love those who love them." (Luke 6:30–32)*

REFLECT: _____

_____

_____

_____

_____

_____

_____

_____

_____

_____

_____

DAY 6   Use the following space to write any thoughts God has put in your heart and mind about the things discussed during session two and/or during your Reflections time this week.

SUMMARY: _____

_____

_____

_____

_____

_____

_____

_____

_____

_____

_____

_____

COMMUNITY-BUILDING SERVICE — NEHEMIAH

It's easy to sometimes feel all alone in your service for the Lord. That's why it is good to experience once in a while the wideness and breadth of the body of Christ so that we do not grow weary in well-doing. Conferences like Promise Keepers and Women of Faith, big Sunday services like Easter and Christmas, and anniversary celebrations confirm our place in a large body of believers who all want to serve God and follow Christ. These experiences are not necessary to faith, but they do help bolster our faith when we can take advantage of them.

Sometimes I wonder about heaven being actually boring, if there is nothing to do but sit around and play harps. That's why I don't believe those folk myths about heaven. Actually, Jesus said if we are faithful in the little things on earth, he will put us in charge of all his possessions in heaven, which sounds like quite a bit of responsibility to me. Imagine what it will be like working with such a grand heavenly team. We need to get this kind of eternal perspective on what we do together in the world today. We are a part of God's army and each one of us is essential to the whole. It's a perspective we can't afford to miss.

CONNECTING WITH GOD'S FAMILY   20 MIN.

Having a vision is one thing—convincing your team to build it is something else. But without their combined abilities, your big audacious goal may never get off the drawing board. In this lesson, we'll consider how we can rally people into action to meet a need, and enjoy the blessings of community more when we work together.

1. What would you be likely to say if your next-door neighbor asked you to help him repair the fence next weekend?

2. Think of a time you were part of a team effort that resulted in achieving a huge goal. What did it take to get the team moving and what was the result of their action?

3. Check in with your spiritual partner(s), or with another partner if yours is absent. Share something God taught you during your time in his Word this week. Be sure to write down your partner's progress on page 93.

GROWING TO BE LIKE CHRIST   40 MIN.

If there was one thing Nehemiah understood, it was the power of influence in accomplishing goals. As cupbearer to King Arta-xerxes, he held one of the highest positions in Persia. Along with his rank came influence, notoriety, and the opportunity to learn how to network, achieve buy-in, and make the right connections.

When Nehemiah heard the news that the walls of Jerusalem lay in ruins and that his people, now reestablishing their lives after years of exile, were being mocked, his heart was broken. In spite of years away, he was still a Jew. That blood connection ran deep.

These people had been in captivity for more than fifty years, Nehemiah realized. They had to be feeling discouraged and with-out hope — maybe even abandoned by God. But they were his people — God's chosen ones. What could he do to remind them of their place in this world? How could he convince them God was still on their side? Nehemiah knew he had to go home and use what God had given him to restore their confidence and dignity.

He sized up the situation, called in some favors based on his many connections, and gathered the people together. There was no time to waste! He pointed out the problem, issued a call to action, explained the benefits, and laid out his vision.

Read Nehemiah 2:17–18:

> Then I said to them, "You see the trouble we are in: Jerusalem lies in ruins, and its gates have been burned with fire. Come, let us rebuild the wall of Jerusalem, and we will no longer be in disgrace." [18]I also told them about the gracious hand of my God upon me and what the king had said to me. They replied, "Let us start rebuilding." So they began this good work.

4. Have someone in your group read Nehemiah 1:3–4. What prompted Nehemiah into action?

5. What was the first thing Nehemiah did after receiving this news?

6. Have you ever had your heart broken by a need? Briefly share your story.

7. Outline the steps Nehemiah took to stir the people of Israel into action in Nehemiah 2:17 – 18. How did they respond? See verse 18b.

8. What do you think Nehemiah understood about his position as a leader?

9. Nehemiah realized that in order to accomplish the task before him, he needed to establish a goal. But he'd never built a wall before. Where do you think this cupbearer found the courage to tackle this job?

10. In what ways do you see Nehemiah as a model for leadership? Make a list.

FOR DEEPER STUDY

Read Nehemiah 6:1–14. All great leaders face opposition sooner or later, and when the work is the Lord's, it's usually sooner.

How did Nehemiah handle his enemies' repeated requests for a meeting? What do you think they really wanted to accomplish, and how did Nehemiah keep them from getting their way?

Note any lessons you see in Nehemiah's leadership style that you want to apply in your own life.

DEVELOPING YOUR GIFTS TO SERVE OTHERS   10 MIN.

Nehemiah understood who his people were — and he saw that they had forgotten *whose* they were. After so many years in captivity, they had lost their compass settings and drifted off course. Someone had to get their attention before it was too late!

11. As a Christ-follower, what responsibility do you think you have for other members of God's family when they are discouraged?

12. How can you be more aware of the needs within your group, family, or church?

13. Nehemiah also understood how to use the talents within his group. What do you see in his example that you could follow in helping other believers develop their God-given abilities?

14. In session two you used the Gifts Inventory and Team Roles sections of the appendix to help you discover your specific gifts and talents you have for serving within your group. Take some time now to plan a group social—a time when you can all get together in an informal setting to share a meal or fun activity. Use your individual talents to make this a special event for your group. This could be a dinner out, a potluck, a night of bowling or going to a movie—whatever you want. Some of you volunteer to plan this event and report your ideas to the group in session five.

SHARING YOUR LIFE MISSION EVERY DAY   10 MIN.

15. Discuss a need you see today in your nation or your community. Is there something your group could do to address this need? How will you be a Nehemiah for your generation?

16. In session one you used the Circles of Life (page 19) to help you identify those around you who might benefit from joining your group. Did you extend an invitation to someone? How was it received? If you haven't asked anyone to join you for this group yet, follow up with that this week.

SURRENDERING YOUR LIFE FOR GOD'S PLEASURE   15–20 MIN.

Even though he had lived a life of relative ease in Artaxerxes' palace, Nehemiah knew who owned his heart and to whom his allegiance belonged. When the needs of his people became known to him, Nehemiah had no trouble surrendering his life to meet that need.

17. Share your prayer requests with the group. Think about the list you made of Nehemiah's leadership qualities in question 10. As you pray for one another, ask God to build those qualities into your life so they are available whenever he calls on you to lead. Record prayer requests on the Prayer and Praise Report provided on page 45. Have any of last week's prayer requests been answered? If so, celebrate those answers to prayer.

18. Use the Reflections verses at the end of this session in your quiet time this week. Record any thoughts or direction you receive from the Lord in the space provided.

STUDY NOTES

What the king had said to me. Nehemiah was in good standing with the king even though he was a Jew in exile. This was also the case for other great Jewish leaders before him, such as Joseph and Daniel. The king was pleased with Nehemiah's service so he was pleased also to let him go (see Nehemiah 2:6). Nehemiah's personal memoirs occupy a large part of the book of Nehemiah, and they reveal him as a man of prayer, action, and devotion to duty.

Let us rebuild the wall. As long as Jerusalem was surrounded by the ruins of a wall, it would be difficult for the city to recapture its past glory. Its inhabitants would have been disheartened. A city wall would begin to restore pride in the city and God. It is important to note that the rebuilding did more to resurrect the people's spiritual lives than their political position. Upon completion of the wall, the Holy Scriptures were brought out and read publicly and the people listened with eagerness in their desire to obey God once again (Nehemiah 8:1–18). And the reading of the Scriptures led to a corporate prayer of repentance (9:1–38).

Briefly share your prayer requests with the large group, making notations below. Then gather in small groups of two to four to pray for each other.

Date: _____

PRAYER REQUESTS

_____

_____

_____

_____

_____

_____

_____

_____

_____

_____

_____

_____

PRAISE REPORT

_____

_____

_____

_____

_____

_____

_____

_____

REFLECTIONS

Each day read the daily verse(s) and give prayerful consideration to what you learn about God, his Spirit, and his place in your life. Then record your thoughts, insights, or prayer in the Reflect section. On day six record a summary of what you have learned over the entire week through this study.

DAY 1   *"When I heard these things, I sat down and wept. For some days I mourned and fasted and prayed before the God of heaven."* (Nehemiah 1:4)

REFLECT: _____

_____

_____

_____

_____

_____

_____

_____

DAY 2   *"But when Sanballat the Horonite, Tobiah the Ammonite official and Geshem the Arab heard about it, they mocked and ridiculed us. 'What is this you are doing?' they asked. 'Are you rebelling against the king?' I answered them by saying, 'The God of heaven will give us success.'"* (Nehemiah 2:19–20)

REFLECT: _____

_____

_____

_____

_____

_____

_____

DAY 3   *"Remember me with favor, O my God, for all I have done for these people."* (Nehemiah 5:19)

REFLECT: _____

_____

_____

_____

_____

_____

_____

_____

_____

_____

DAY 4   *"All the believers were one in heart and mind. No one claimed that any of his possessions was his own, but they shared everything they had. . . . There were no needy persons among them. For from time to time those who owned lands or houses sold them, brought the money from the sales and put it at the apostles' feet, and it was distributed to anyone as he had need."* (Acts 4:32, 34–35)

REFLECT: _____

_____

_____

_____

_____

_____

_____

_____

_____

_____

_____

DAY 5 *"So the Twelve gathered all the disciples together and said, 'It would not be right for us to neglect the ministry of the word of God in order to wait on tables. Brothers, choose seven men from among you who are known to be full of the Spirit and wisdom. We will turn this responsibility over to them and will give our attention to prayer and the ministry of the word.' This proposal pleased the whole group."* (Acts 6:2–5)

REFLECT: _____

_____

_____

_____

_____

_____

_____

_____

_____

_____

DAY 6 Use the following space to write any thoughts God has put in your heart and mind about the things discussed during session three and/ or during your Reflections time this week.

SUMMARY: _____

_____

_____

_____

_____

_____

_____

_____

_____

_____

_____

_____

OBEDIENT SERVICE — NOAH

As a writer, I have always wanted to write the great American novel. I had a good deal of nonfiction under my belt, but fiction was very intimidating. How do good novelists create those complex story lines they come up with and all the nuances of characters and layered meanings underneath the plot? For the longest time I put off starting a story, thinking you had to have all the information before you started. Then I suddenly felt God urging me to just start. Start? Start with what? And then I experienced a scene in real life where I could see a character that inspired me, if I began with that one scene and followed where it might lead. (A little like Abraham striking out for a land he did not know anything about.)

It's a risky proposition, but in the end it worked. Even choices I made early on that seemed arbitrary at the time turned into important pieces of the whole. The more I worked with this process, the more I realized how much like life it is. God cannot reveal the whole story to us before we start out. He can only let us see it bit by bit as we live. But each day, we discover a deeper significance of that which we found earlier. It's the way faith grows; and it's the way we gain more courage to believe and act. So I guess you could say, we're all novelists of sorts. Just imagine what this story is going to look like when it's done!

CONNECTING WITH GOD'S FAMILY   20 MIN.

God-assignments can often seem overwhelming and confusing — until we remember who is really in charge. With God, we don't have to have it all figured out in advance. In this session, we'll look at Noah and how he tackled Ark Building 101. When we put our trust in God to use our abilities, even when we don't fully understand the assignment, it's amazing what often results.

1. When you receive an assignment, do you typically dig right in or procrastinate?

49

2. Talk about a time you were given a job to do with little or no instruction on how to do it. How was the assignment completed?

3. Check in with your spiritual partner(s), or with another partner if yours is absent. Share with your partner(s) your progress in working on the goal you set for yourself last week. What obstacles hindered you from following through? Make a note about your partner's progress and how you can pray for him or her this week.

GROWING TO BE LIKE CHRIST   40 MIN.

An ark? What's an ark? Rain? I've never heard of such a thing! Noah had to have wondered. But God was insistent, and Noah knew better than to argue with the Almighty. So he listened, and God gave him what he needed to accomplish the task before him. He listened, and God told him what he was about to do.

Floodwaters covering the earth? All life destroyed? Noah's heart clutched in his chest. But he listened, and God took away his fear. "With you, Noah," God said, "it will be different." Noah had found favor in God's eyes.

Noah listened and God told him to bring a male and female of every type of creature on the earth into the ark. Imagine that wildlife expedition! In addition to building the first ark, Noah must have organized the world's first safari. God also told Noah that the animals were not to be used for food, but to bring every other kind of food available onto the ark and store it up for his family's and the animals' use. And this was long before the discount warehouse!

Finally, we read in verse 22 that Noah knew how to follow directions. He faithfully accomplished everything God had told him to do, just as God had instructed.

Read Genesis 6:14–22:

> "So make yourself an ark of cypress wood; make rooms in it and coat it with pitch inside and out. ¹⁵This is how you are

to build it: The ark is to be 450 feet long, 75 feet wide and 45 feet high. ¹⁶Make a roof for it and finish the ark to within 18 inches of the top. Put a door in the side of the ark and make lower, middle and upper decks. ¹⁷I am going to bring floodwaters on the earth to destroy all life under the heavens, every creature that has the breath of life in it. Everything on earth will perish. ¹⁸But I will establish my covenant with you, and you will enter the ark—you and your sons and your wife and your sons' wives with you. ¹⁹You are to bring into the ark two of all living creatures, male and female, to keep them alive with you. ²⁰Two of every kind of bird, of every kind of animal and of every kind of creature that moves along the ground will come to you to be kept alive. ²¹You are to take every kind of food that is to be eaten and store it away as food for you and for them." ²²Noah did everything just as God commanded him.

4. What did God give Noah (see verses 14–16)?

5. Noah was being asked by God to do something that had never been done before. God knew he needed instructions, and he supplied them. Though Scripture doesn't tell us, how do you think Noah prepared his heart to hear God's detailed directions?

6. Was Noah any different from you? What can you do to hear God's voice more clearly?

7. God often asks us to do extraordinary things for him even when we don't have it all figured out. Whether or not we understand, God wants us to "just start building." How do you typically respond when you receive an unclear

assignment? What if the people directing your project either fail to or are not able to offer the guidance you desire?

8. Based on Genesis 6:22, how important do you think it is to obey God completely?

9. How can we follow Noah's example today?

FOR DEEPER STUDY

Read Genesis 6:1–7. What was God preparing to do and why?

Now stop for a minute on the next verse, Genesis 6:8. What does it say about Noah?

Our times are much like the days of Noah. How can we live in them in such a way that we also find favor in God's eyes?

DEVELOPING YOUR GIFTS TO SERVE OTHERS   10 MIN.

10. While we don't know for certain what Noah's God-given talents were, it's likely he was good at working with his hands

and at building things. How could acknowledging your God-given abilities and investing regularly in their development help you be ready to "build an ark" when God hands you that assignment?

11. Do you think it matters if you don't always understand how God is going to use what you are doing? Why or why not? How can this perspective give you confidence in serving others for Christ's sake?

12. Consider what's next for your group. Don't wait until the last minute to prayerfully consider what God wants your group to do after you finish this study. Spend a few minutes looking to the future and discussing that as a group.

 SHARING YOUR LIFE MISSION EVERY DAY   10 MIN.

Imagine you had to go round up a pair of every kind of animal on earth and load them onto the ark. God-assignments are not necessarily easy. But because of Noah's obedience, all mankind has had the opportunity to be saved.

13. How can you be a Noah in your generation? Is there a mission you sense God is calling you to pursue?

14. Think about a couple of steps you could take this week toward accomplishing that mission.

15. Noah could not fully understand what God had in mind, but because he trusted God he willingly surrendered his abilities for God's use. Does God have access right now to your abilities? If you've been having difficulty trusting God to direct your future, ask your group to pray with you for ark-building-type faith. In simple, one-sentence prayers take a few moments to thank God for his commitment to your growth.

16. Look ahead to session six, question 13 in the Surrendering section (page 77). We suggest that you create a special moment to close this study, celebrating the servant heart of your group by having a footwashing. Make plans now; maybe several of you can share in providing supplies. Find guidelines for performing a footwashing on pages 104–105 of the appendix.

17. Use the Reflections verses at the end of this session in your quiet time this week. Record any thoughts or direction you receive from the Lord in the space provided.

STUDY NOTES

But I will establish my covenant with you. The covenant spoken of here is most likely the one God made with Noah after the flood: that he would never again destroy all flesh with a flood. As such, it was universal, applying to every living creature; it was unconditional; and it was everlasting.

Everything on earth will perish. This shows how far the moral condition of humanity had fallen in such a relatively short time.

Finish the ark to within 18 inches of the top. This was an open area just under the roofline to allow for light and air.

Two of every kind ... will come to you. This shows how God cooperated with Noah. There really was a procession of animals as so many pictorial interpretations have it. The animals came to the ark, two by two, under their own will, as directed by God. It is interesting to note that the animals came, but the people did not.

Noah did everything just as God commanded him. Noah was 480 years old when God commanded him to build the ark, 500 when his first son was born, and 600 when the flood came. That means God gave the people 120 years of grace, during which time Noah preached, but there was no repentance. He was 950 when he died. This longevity is consistent with the patriarchs of this period prior to the flood, but it also indicates something about the longevity of God's mercy. He gave people more than ample time to believe in his salvation.

PRAYER AND PRAISE REPORT

Briefly share your prayer requests with the large group, making notations below. Then gather in small groups of two to four to pray for each other.

Date: _____

PRAYER REQUESTS

_____

_____

_____

_____

_____

_____

_____

_____

_____

_____

_____

PRAISE REPORT

_____

_____

_____

_____

_____

_____

_____

_____

REFLECTIONS

Each day read the daily verse(s) and give prayerful consideration to what you learn about God, his Spirit, and his place in your life. Then record your thoughts, insights, or prayer in the Reflect section. On day six record a summary of what you have learned over the entire week through this study.

DAY 1   *"When you pass through the waters, I will be with you; and when you pass through the rivers, they will not sweep over you. When you walk through the fire, you will not be burned; the flames will not set you ablaze." (Isaiah 43:2)*

REFLECT: _____

_____

_____

_____

_____

_____

_____

_____

_____

DAY 2   *"Then I said, 'Here I am — it is written about me in the scroll — I have come to do your will, O God.'" (Hebrews 10:7)*

REFLECT: _____

_____

_____

_____

_____

_____

_____

_____

DAY 3   *"My son, keep my words and store up my commands within you. Keep my commands and you will live; guard my teachings as the apple of your eye. Bind them on your fingers; write them on the tablet of your heart." (Proverbs 7:1–3)*

REFLECT: _____

_____

_____

_____

_____

_____

_____

_____

_____

_____

DAY 4   *"You know that the household of Stephanas were the first converts in Achaia, and they have devoted themselves to the service of the saints. I urge you, brothers, to submit to such as these and to everyone who joins in the work, and labors at it." (1 Corinthians 16:15–16)*

REFLECT: _____

_____

_____

_____

_____

_____

_____

_____

_____

DAY 5   *"I can do everything through him who gives me strength."*
(Philippians 4:13)

REFLECT: _____

_____

_____

_____

_____

_____

_____

_____

_____

_____

_____

_____

_____

DAY 6   Use the following space to write any thoughts God has put in your heart and mind about the things discussed during session four and/or during your Reflections time this week.

SUMMARY: _____

_____

_____

_____

_____

_____

_____

_____

_____

_____

_____

_____

_____

TIMELY SERVICE — ESTHER

As a speaker who has traveled extensively, I have been fortunate to be able to see my prophetic gift utilized at a number of significant moments. My gifts are such that I actually long for crisis situations because it is then that God gives me specific unction and the confidence to know a message is from him, along with the boldness to speak it. Like the time I was scheduled to deliver a chapel talk at a Christian college on the day after 9/11. As if that were not enough impetus, my daughter was a student at that college and rooting for me from the front row! As you can imagine, I couldn't wait to get going, because I knew that God had prepared me and put me there for such a time as this.

We all have gifts that will be called into use in timely situations. The way you know you are ready for this is the confidence level you have. That doesn't mean you won't have some fear and trembling as well — that usually comes along with the package — but the confidence you have will be strong enough to overcome all obstacles. These are times when our faith rises to the surface, and we experience the Holy Spirit's power firsthand. As you can imagine, these times are great faith-builders and can leave us with something to take to heart during the less glamorous day in, day out of life.

CONNECTING WITH GOD'S FAMILY   20 MIN.

In a world full of competition and crowds everywhere we go, it seems odd to consider that any one of us could ever be "the only one." But every now and then, an assignment comes along with just one person's name on it. Such was the case for Esther. Because of her position, Esther was uniquely placed to save her people from the death sentence they faced. In this session we'll consider the decision Esther had to make, how she prepared herself to take a stand, and how we can be an Esther in our time.

1. How do you respond when you are singled out for an assignment?

2. Share a time when you spoke up for what is right, or a time when you should have spoken up and didn't. What happened?

3. Check in with your spiritual partner(s), or with another partner if yours is absent. Share how your quiet time went this week, or read a brief section from your journal if you're keeping one. Be sure to write down your partner's progress on page 93.

4. How is your event planning going? Update everyone now on the status of your upcoming group social.

GROWING TO BE LIKE CHRIST   40 MIN.

Mordecai was distraught. Haman, the king's second-in-command, managed to persuade King Xerxes to issue an edict that all Jews in the kingdom be killed. And all because Mordecai refused to pay Haman allegiance. *What a self-centered man* ... but this was no time for grumbling. What could be done to save his people?

Esther! Mordecai thought of his niece, the beautiful young woman who had recently become the king's bride. Of course — it was the only way. She was a Jew as well!

Even your life is on the line, Mordecai wrote her. *If you stay silent, God will save his people some other way — we have his word on it! But Esther, I have no doubt you and your father's family will perish in the genocide. Perhaps, dear Esther, God has given you the position you currently have for just this purpose. Is it not possible that you have been hand-selected by God to save your people?*

Stunned by the news and the stark reality of her choice, Esther immediately issued a request. *Ask all the Jews to fast on my behalf,* she wrote back to Mordecai. *My servants and I will do the same. After three days, I will go to the king, even though his law forbids it. Whatever happens then, we must accept.*

On the third day, Esther dressed up in her finest robes and respectfully approached the king, coming just close enough to make her presence known. Her heart pounded as she waited to see what he would do. Xerxes summoned her to come to him — a good sign. Clearly, he loved his queen.

"What can I do for you? Just name it!" he said. Another hopeful sign.

For Esther, it was now or never. She summoned her courage, drew in a deep breath, and spoke. "Will you and Haman come to a banquet I've prepared for you?" she asked. It was a simple act, but it set the stage for what God was about to do.

Read Esther 4:13–17; 5:1–4:

> He [Mordecai] sent back this answer: "Do not think that because you are in the king's house you alone of all the Jews will escape. ¹⁴For if you remain silent at this time, relief and deliverance for the Jews will arise from another place, but you and your father's family will perish. And who knows but that you have come to royal position for such a time as this?" ¹⁵Then Esther sent this reply to Mordecai: ¹⁶"Go, gather together all the Jews who are in Susa, and fast for me. Do not eat or drink for three days, night or day. I and my maids will fast as you do. When this is done, I will go to the king, even though it is against the law. And if I perish, I perish." ¹⁷So Mordecai went away and carried out all of Esther's instructions.
>
> ⁵:¹On the third day Esther put on her royal robes and stood in the inner court of the palace, in front of the king's hall. The king was sitting on his royal throne in the hall, facing the entrance. ²When he saw Queen Esther standing in the court, he was pleased with her and held out to her the gold scepter that was in his hand. So Esther approached and touched the tip of the scepter. ³Then the king asked, "What is it, Queen Esther? What is your request? Even up to half the kingdom, it will be given you." ⁴"If it pleases the king," replied Esther, "let the king, together with Haman, come today to a banquet I have prepared for him."

5. Have someone in your group read Esther 2:17. What do you see in this verse that tells you God had a plan to rescue his people?

6. It's interesting to note that God is never mentioned by name in the entire book of Esther. Yet Mordecai is certain the Jewish people will somehow be delivered (Esther 4:14). Where do you think his confidence came from?

7. How does Esther's decision to go to the king on behalf of her nation (Esther 4:16) stand out against typical choices people make?

8. Esther asked that her people fast and pray for her as she prepared herself for what she was about to do. How important is the support of your group to you when you take on a God-assignment?

9. What do you think of the fact that Esther fasted and prayed too?

10. Esther's attitude toward the king is especially noted in Esther 5:1–4. Why does our attitude matter as we approach those with whom God has appointed us to work?

11. What one character quality about Esther speaks most to you as a believer? Go around the group and make a list of what each person says. (There are NO wrong answers!)

12. The story of Esther is often chosen as an example of recognizing our moment in history. How does Esther typify the need to be ready to act when God calls on us?

13. Share a story of an Esther moment in your life or in the life of someone you know or have heard about.

FOR DEEPER STUDY

Read the rest of Esther's story (through Esther 10). Make a list of all the intersections where you see God's hand in delivering his people. How does what you see clarify Esther's singular role?

DEVELOPING YOUR GIFTS TO SERVE OTHERS   15 MIN.

Esther was likely motivated to action by her desire to save herself and her people from destruction. She trusted that God's will would prevail, so she acted in faith. Esther had her priorities straight. King Xerxes welcomed Esther into his court.

14. How can another person's response to us be an indication of our purpose? Think about times when the pleasure your work brought to someone else helped you choose a life goal or direction.

15. To be available for God's work, we must understand what our priorities are and set them appropriately. Self-examination is a valuable step toward accomplishing this, and it often reveals things we don't expect to find. Prayerfully work through the following exercises. Ask God to reveal any area he wants to highlight for growth in your life.

Area for growth:

- **List the top five things you believe are most important to you.**

Area for growth:

- When your mind is free to wander, where do your thoughts go? **What fills much of your thought life?**

Area for growth:

- Think about your calendar and your daily schedule. **How do you spend most of your time?**

Area for growth:

- Think about your finances. **Where are the top five places your money goes?**

Has God highlighted an area in which you need to see some changes? Share with the group one area God is urging you to grow in at this time. Consider asking the group or your spiritual partner to hold you accountable for your next step of growth.

16. What we think about and how we spend our time and money are very good indicators of what is most important

to us. The sad reality is that too frequently what we *say* we believe is important to us just doesn't match up with the evidence. How do you think this might affect our ability to see God's will for our lives?

SHARING YOUR LIFE MISSION EVERY DAY   5 MIN.

Esther's choice to serve God by stepping out in faith for her people required a huge decision. She literally put her life on the line.

17. What do you think Esther saw as her mission?

18. In session two you began planning a project or ministry you could serve in together as an outreach to your community. Report the status of this planned effort for the group now. What do you plan to do, and when?

SURRENDERING YOUR LIFE FOR GOD'S PLEASURE   15–20 MIN.

Is there a place where God is calling you to be an Esther? What would it take for you to make the kind of decision Esther made? As a group, pray for one another to have the courage to stand up for God's people whenever a choice must be made.

19. Before you leave, allow everyone to answer this question: How can we pray for you this week? Be sure to write these requests on your Prayer and Praise Report on page 69 and close your meeting by praying for these requests. Commit to continue praying for each other throughout the week.

20. Use the Reflections verses at the end of this session in your quiet time this week. Record any thoughts or direction you receive from the Lord in the space provided.

STUDY NOTES

Then Esther sent this reply to Mordecai. Both Esther and Mordecai are examples of how God honors his people in the midst of Jewish exile and domination by pagan kings. (Daniel, Shadrach, Meshach, Abednego, and Nehemiah are others.) Because of their faithfulness and their position, the children of Israel in their generation were saved and protected.

For if you remain silent at this time, relief and deliverance for the Jews will arise from another place. God's will being done does not depend on our cooperation, but we can be a part of his plan if we choose to go along with it, no matter what the cost.

Do not eat or drink for three days. Fasting in the Old Testament generally meant going without all food and drink for a period of time. It was done ceremonially on certain allotted days such as the Day of Atonement, and on other days as a sign of grief, penitence, or, as in this case, a humbling before God for the purpose of securing his guidance and help. But fasting does not guarantee results. Without right conduct, it is in vain (Isaiah 58:5–12).

I will go to the king, even though it is against the law. It was not the custom of the time for the queen to initiate anything with the king, even a hearing before him.

Haman. The villain of this story who was plotting to massacre the Jews when his vanity was hurt by Mordecai's refusal to bow to him (a position reserved only for the one true God). When his manipulations were finally revealed to the king, he was hanged on the very gallows he had prepared for Mordecai.

So Esther approached and touched the tip of the scepter. An ornate staff or rod borne as a symbol of personal sovereignty or authority. In touching the king's scepter, Esther was recognizing and respecting his kingly position.

Briefly share your prayer requests with the large group, making notations below. Then gather in small groups of two to four to pray for each other.

Date: _____

PRAYER REQUESTS

_____

_____

_____

_____

_____

_____

_____

_____

_____

_____

_____

_____

PRAISE REPORT

_____

_____

_____

_____

_____

_____

_____

_____

_____

69

REFLECTIONS

Each day read the daily verse(s) and give prayerful consideration to what you learn about God, his Spirit, and his place in your life. Then record your thoughts, insights, or prayer in the Reflect section. On day six record a summary of what you have learned over the entire week through this study.

DAY 1   *"So then, King Agrippa, I was not disobedient to the vision from heaven. First to those in Damascus, then to those in Jerusalem and in all Judea, and to the Gentiles also, I preached that they should repent and turn to God and prove their repentance by their deeds."* (Acts 26:19–20)

REFLECT: _____

_____

_____

_____

_____

_____

_____

_____

DAY 2   *"For if you remain silent at this time, relief and deliverance for the Jews will arise from another place, but you and your father's family will perish. And who knows but that you have come to royal position for such a time as this?"* (Esther 4:14)

REFLECT: _____

_____

_____

_____

_____

_____

_____

_____

DAY 3   *"Sow your seed in the morning, and at evening let not your hands be idle, for you do not know which will succeed, whether this or that, or whether both will do equally well." (Ecclesiastes 11:6)*

REFLECT: _____

_____

_____

_____

_____

_____

_____

_____

_____

DAY 4   *"Show me, O LORD, my life's end and the number of my days; let me know how fleeting is my life. You have made my days a mere handbreadth; the span of my years is as nothing before you. Each man's life is but a breath. Man is a mere phantom as he goes to and fro: He bustles about, but only in vain; he heaps up wealth, not knowing who will get it. But now, Lord, what do I look for? My hope is in you." (Psalm 39:4–7)*

REFLECT: _____

_____

_____

_____

_____

_____

_____

_____

_____

DAY 5 *"Then I heard the voice of the Lord saying, 'Whom shall I send? And who will go for us?' And I said, 'Here am I. Send me!'"* (Isaiah 6:8)

REFLECT: _____

_____

_____

_____

_____

_____

_____

_____

_____

_____

_____

DAY 6 Use the following space to write any thoughts God has put in your heart and mind about the things discussed during session five and/or during your Reflections time this week.

SUMMARY: _____

_____

_____

_____

_____

_____

_____

_____

_____

_____

_____

GIANT SERVICE — DAVID

My wife was seven months pregnant at the time and we were staying in a hotel a thousand miles from our home along with a family friend who was serving as nanny for our eighteen-month-old son. We were playing a game of Hearts in our hotel room one night when my wife threw out the Queen of Spades and said, "Uh-oh!" Thinking she had mistakenly led with the Queen, our friend and I smiled because we sensed this was a chance to set her back from the substantial lead she held in the game right then. We thought nothing more of it until she stood up and revealed the true nature of her concern. Her water had broken.

Panic ensued. Actually, my wife was the calmest, telling us matter-of-factly what to do. At 8:30 the next morning, at a nearby hospital, our daughter was born and, at a little over four pounds, was placed in an incubator for the next five weeks. During that time, an incredible sense of guidance took hold of me as God led me to a temporary apartment for us, and a means of continuing my responsibilities that had precipitated this trip away from home. Confident decision making is not my usual cup of tea, but this time I had God's strength for each decision. It was such a time that I felt literally buoyed by my faith. Though I wish I could continue this level of faith activity all the time, I did have it when I needed it, and that experience continues to remind me of what I need even in lesser crises. Once you slay one giant, you come to welcome the next.

CONNECTING WITH GOD'S FAMILY   20 MIN.

Now and then an obstacle comes along that looks too big for us to handle. That's when we need a new point of view, like the one David offered when Israel needed a champion to go against the Philistine giant, Goliath. In this final session, we'll examine the legendary battle between the towering Goliath and the undersized shepherd boy with a slingshot and a pouchful of pebbles. Where can you be a David against a Goliath in your world?

What an uneven match: huge, grizzly, professional Goliath against a raw rookie shepherd boy. King Saul was skeptical when the

young court musician came to him, pleading to be given the opportunity. They had scoured the kingdom looking for a suitable opponent to take on Goliath, and here comes this unlikely candidate. David was four feet too short, fifteen years too young, and didn't have proper training. What he *did* have was a God-sized faith.

1. Share a time when you had a job you thought could not be done. How did it go?

2. What difference do you think a positive attitude makes when taking on any assignment?

3. Check in with your spiritual partner(s), or with another partner if yours is absent. During this last session, share a final update on your growth progress over the past weeks. Record yours and your partner's progress on page 93.

GROWING TO BE LIKE CHRIST   40 MIN.

Goliath could hardly believe his eyes — was this a joke these Israelites were playing on him? They told him they had a soldier to fight him — but this was no soldier. It was a mere boy, and a shepherd boy at that! What was he doing over there by the stream?

This wasn't going to be pretty, but he might as well get it over with. Goliath stomped toward David. "Come here, little man, and let me feed you to the birds!" Goliath shouted. But he hadn't counted on David having an accomplice — and a Mighty One at that.

"You've got mighty weapons," David called back, "but I've got One that's bigger than any you can devise. I come in the name of the Lord Almighty, the God of Israel. He's the One you made fun of, remember? That wasn't a smart decision."

Imagine the scene as someone literally half his size challenges this immense brute. But David put his complete confidence in God as he ran forward to meet his enemy.

Read 1 Samuel 17:40–48:

*Then he took his staff in his hand, chose five smooth stones
from the stream, put them in the pouch of his shepherd's bag
and, with his sling in his hand, approached the Philistine.
⁴¹Meanwhile, the Philistine, with his shield bearer in front of
him, kept coming closer to David. ⁴²He looked David over
and saw that he was only a boy, ruddy and handsome, and
he despised him. ⁴³He said to David, "Am I a dog, that you
come at me with sticks?" And the Philistine cursed David by
his gods. ⁴⁴"Come here," he said, "and I'll give your flesh to
the birds of the air and the beasts of the field!"*

*⁴⁵David said to the Philistine, "You come against me with
sword and spear and javelin, but I come against you in the
name of the LORD Almighty, the God of the armies of Israel,
whom you have defied. ⁴⁶This day the LORD will hand you
over to me, and I'll strike you down and cut off your head.
Today I will give the carcasses of the Philistine army to the
birds of the air and the beasts of the earth, and the whole
world will know that there is a God in Israel. ⁴⁷All those gathered here will know that it is not by sword or spear that the
LORD saves; for the battle is the LORD's, and he will give all of
you into our hands." ⁴⁸As the Philistine moved closer to attack
him, David ran quickly toward the battle line to meet him.*

4. In 1 Samuel 17:40, God takes time to tell us that David
   chose five smooth stones from the stream. As a shepherd,
   what might David's experience be, and how does this speak
   to you about using what God has given you to serve him?

5. When the Israelites looked at Goliath, they saw a fearsome
   enemy. How do you think David viewed Goliath?

6. What do you think gave David this unique perspective?

7. Even though David was skilled with the slingshot, what do you read in verses 45–47 that tells you his confidence was not in his own abilities?

8. Why do we tend to think success or failure in any given task depends on our ability to do the job?

9. How can this lesson from the life of David make a difference for you the next time you are in a situation that looks too big to handle?

FOR DEEPER STUDY

Read 1 Samuel 17, beginning with verse 20. What additional qualities do you see in young David that you think may have contributed to his victory over Goliath?

In overcoming obstacles in our lives, how much do you think depends on us and how much depends on God?

DEVELOPING YOUR GIFTS TO SERVE OTHERS   10 MIN.

When we consider the life of David, we find a multifaceted man — shepherd, musician, poet, and king. But he never forgot his shepherd training. Let's consider for a moment what we can learn from David about growing our abilities to serve.

10. God's will was accomplished because David saw the situation from God's perspective. What could help you develop your ability to see life through God's eyes?

11. Based on your answer to question 10, what step will you take this week to grow in gaining God's perspective?

12. If your group still needs to make decisions about continuing to meet after this session, have that discussion now. Review the Small Group Agreement and consider any adjustments you would like to make before you begin a new study. Decide what you will study next. We recommend another study from our Building Character Together series.

SHARING YOUR LIFE MISSION EVERY DAY   5 MIN.

13. Sometimes when we are sharing Christ, or desiring to share Christ, with others, we can see their resistance to our message as a giant-sized obstacle. What can we learn from this story of David's life that would help us take on those giants with greater confidence? Put your resolve to be like David to the test and knock down a giant or two.

SURRENDERING YOUR LIFE FOR GOD'S PLEASURE   20–25 MIN.

Where in your life do you need David's point of view today? If you are currently facing a Goliath-sized giant, share your story with the group. Go to God in prayer together and ask him for the same assurance he gave David all those years ago.

14. As a demonstration of your commitment to serving one another, experience a time of footwashing together. Instructions can be found in the appendix on pages 104–105. This activity will take some forethought and planning to make it special.

15. Share your prayer requests and record them on the Prayer and Praise Report provided on page 80. Have any previous prayer requests been answered? If so, celebrate those answers. Then, in simple, one-sentence prayers, submit your requests to God and close by thanking him for his commitment to you and for how he has used this group to bring spiritual growth.

16. Use the Reflections verses at the end of this session in your quiet time this week. Record any thoughts or direction you receive from the Lord in the space provided.

STUDY NOTES

Philistines. Throughout the period that Israel was ruled by judges and by kings, the Philistines gave the nation continual problems. The Scriptures go so far as to say that God used the Philistines to test the Israelites (Judges 3:1–3). At their worst, the Israelites adopted their gods (10:6–7); at their best, they were victorious over them (Samson and David).

Goliath. Goliath was a formidable enemy. He was nine feet tall. He wore a bronze helmet and bronze shin guards, his coat of armor alone weighed 125 pounds, and the javelin he had slung over his back had an iron point that weighed over fifteen pounds. Goliath had been taunting the armies of Israel for forty days, coming out each day and challenging someone to fight him. David was there only because his father sent him with some food for his older brothers in the battle. When he got there on the fortieth day, David couldn't believe they were letting this go on when God was on their side (1 Samuel 17:26).

David. David was the youngest son of Jesse. God told Samuel to go to the house of Jesse and anoint one of his sons as Israel's king. Jesse let seven of his sons pass before Samuel and yet God did not confirm any of them in Samuel's heart. That's when Samuel asked Jesse if he had any more sons. Yes, his youngest son, David, was out tending sheep. No one had even considered David because he was but a lad. Samuel sent for him and knew right away that this was God's choice (1 Samuel 16:1–12), thus confirming again how God's choices are rarely ours.

And the whole world will know that there is a God in Israel. David's strength came straight from his faith. He knew no one could taunt God and get away with it. He had already rejected the armor Saul tried to put on him. (It was too big.) He knew his strength was only in one place: in the Lord.

Briefly share your prayer requests with the large group, making notations below. Then gather in small groups of two to four to pray for each other.

Date: _____

PRAYER REQUESTS

_____
_____
_____
_____
_____
_____
_____
_____
_____
_____
_____
_____

PRAISE REPORT

_____
_____
_____
_____
_____
_____
_____
_____
_____

REFLECTIONS

Each day read the daily verse(s) and give prayerful consideration to what you learn about God, his Spirit, and his place in your life. Then record your thoughts, insights, or prayer in the Reflect section. On day six record a summary of what you have learned over the entire week through this study.

DAY 1   *"Jesus looked at them and said, 'With man this is impossible, but with God all things are possible.'" (Matthew 19:26)*

REFLECT: _____

_____

_____

_____

_____

_____

_____

_____

_____

_____

DAY 2   *"I am the LORD, the God of all mankind. Is anything too hard for me?" (Jeremiah 32:27)*

REFLECT: _____

_____

_____

_____

_____

_____

_____

_____

_____

_____

DAY 3   *"The LORD is slow to anger and great in power; the LORD will not leave the guilty unpunished. His way is in the whirlwind and the storm, and clouds are the dust of his feet." (Nahum 1:3)*

REFLECT: _____

_____

_____

_____

_____

_____

_____

_____

_____

_____

_____

_____

_____

DAY 4   *"The LORD gives strength to his people; the LORD blesses his people with peace." (Psalm 29:11)*

REFLECT: _____

_____

_____

_____

_____

_____

_____

_____

_____

_____

_____

_____

_____

DAY 5   *"But blessed is the man who trusts in the LORD, whose confidence is in him. He will be like a tree planted by the water that sends out its roots by the stream. It does not fear when heat comes; its leaves are always green. It has no worries in a year of drought and never fails to bear fruit." (Jeremiah 17:7–8)*

REFLECT: _____

_____

_____

_____

_____

_____

_____

_____

_____

_____

_____

_____

DAY 6   Use the following space to write any thoughts God has put in your heart and mind about the things discussed during session six and/or during your Reflections time this week.

SUMMARY: _____

_____

_____

_____

_____

_____

_____

_____

_____

_____

_____

_____

APPENDIX

FREQUENTLY ASKED QUESTIONS

WHAT DO WE DO ON THE FIRST NIGHT OF OUR GROUP?

Like all fun things in life — have a party! A "get to know you" coffee, dinner, or dessert is a great way to launch a new study. You may want to review the Small Group Agreement (pages 89–90) and share the names of a few friends you can invite to join you. But most importantly, have fun before your study time begins.

WHERE DO WE FIND NEW MEMBERS FOR OUR GROUP?

This can be troubling, especially for new groups that have only a few people or for existing groups that lose a few people along the way. We encourage you to pray with your group and then brainstorm a list of people from work, church, your neighborhood, your children's school, family, the gym, and so forth. Then have each group member invite several of the people on his or her list. Another good strategy is to ask church leaders to make an announcement or allow a bulletin insert.

No matter how you find members, it's vital that you stay on the lookout for new people to join your group. All groups tend to go through healthy attrition — the result of moves, releasing new leaders, ministry opportunities, and so forth — and if the group gets too small, it could be at risk of shutting down. If you and your group stay open, you'll be amazed at the people God sends your way. The next person just might become a friend for life. You never know!

HOW LONG WILL THIS GROUP MEET?

It's totally up to the group — once you come to the end of this six-week study. Most groups meet weekly for at least their first six weeks, but every other week can work as well. We strongly recommend that the group meet for the first six months on a weekly basis if at all possible. This allows for continuity, and if people miss a meeting they aren't gone for a whole month.

At the end of this study, each group member may decide if he or she wants to continue on for another six-week study. Some groups launch relationships for years to come, and others are stepping-stones into another group experience. Either way, enjoy the journey.

CAN WE DO THIS STUDY ON OUR OWN?

Absolutely! This may sound crazy but one of the best ways to do this study is not with a full house but with a few friends. You may choose to gather with one other couple who would enjoy going to the movies or having a quiet dinner and then walking through this study. Jesus will be with you even if there are only two of you (Matthew 18:20).

WHAT IF THIS GROUP IS NOT WORKING FOR US?

You're not alone! This could be the result of a personality conflict, life stage difference, geographical distance, level of spiritual maturity, or any number of things. Relax. Pray for God's direction, and at the end of this six-week study, decide whether to continue with this group or find another. You don't buy the first car you look at or marry the first person you date, and the same goes with a group. Don't bail out before the six weeks are up — God might have something to teach you. Also, don't run from conflict or prejudge people before you have given them a chance. God is still working in you too!

WHO IS THE LEADER?

Most groups have an official leader. But ideally, the group will mature and members will rotate the leadership of meetings. We have discovered that healthy groups rotate hosts/leaders and homes on a regular basis. This model ensures that all members grow, give their unique contribution, and develop their gifts. This study guide and the Holy Spirit can keep things on track even when you rotate leaders. Christ has promised to be in your midst as you gather. Ultimately, God is your leader each step of the way.

HOW DO WE HANDLE THE CHILD-CARE NEEDS IN OUR GROUP?

Very carefully. Seriously, this can be a sensitive issue. We suggest that you empower the group to openly brainstorm solutions. You may try one option that works for a while and then adjust over time. Our favorite approach is for adults to meet in the living room or dining room, and to share the cost of a babysitter (or two) who can be with the kids in a different part of the house. In this way, parents don't have to be away from their children all evening when their children are too young to be left at home. A second option is to use one home for the kids and a second home (close by or a phone call away) for the adults. A third idea is to rotate the responsibility of providing a lesson or care for the children either in the same home or in another home nearby. This can be an incredible blessing for kids. Finally, the most common idea is to decide that you need to have a night to invest in your spiritual lives individually or as a couple, and to make your own arrangements for child care. No matter what decision the group makes, the best approach is to dialogue openly about both the problem and the solution.

SMALL GROUP AGREEMENT

OUR PURPOSE

To transform our spiritual lives by cultivating our spiritual health in a healthy small group community. In addition, we: _____

_____

_____

_____

OUR VALUES

Group Attendance	To give priority to the group meeting. We will call or email if we will be late or absent. (Completing the Small Group Calendar on page 91 will minimize this issue.)
Safe Environment	To help create a safe place where people can be heard and feel loved. (Please, no quick answers, snap judgments, or simple fixes.)
Respect Differences	To be gentle and gracious to people with different spiritual maturity, personal opinions, temperaments, or imperfections. We are all works in progress.
Confidentiality	To keep anything that is shared strictly confidential and within the group, and to avoid sharing improper information about those outside the group.
Encouragement for Growth	To be not just takers but givers of life. We want to spiritually multiply our life by serving others with our God-given gifts.

Welcome for Newcomers	To keep an open chair and share Jesus' dream of finding a shepherd for every sheep.
Shared Ownership	To remember that every member is a minister and to ensure that each attender will share a small team role or responsibility over time. (See the Team Roles on pages 98–100.)
Rotating Hosts/Leaders and Homes	To encourage different people to host the group in their homes, and to rotate the responsibility of facilitating each meeting. (See the Small Group Calendar on page 91.)

OUR EXPECTATIONS

- Refreshments/mealtimes _____
- Child care _____
- When we will meet (day of week) _____
- Where we will meet (place) _____
- We will begin at (time) _____ and end at _____
- We will do our best to have some or all of us attend a worship service together. Our primary worship service time will be _____
- Date of this agreement _____
- Date we will review this agreement again _____
- Who (other than the leader) will review this agreement at the end of this study _____

SMALL GROUP CALENDAR

Planning and calendaring can help ensure the greatest participation at every meeting. At the end of each meeting, review this calendar. Be sure to include a regular rotation of host homes and leaders, and don't forget birthdays, socials, church events, holidays, and mission/ministry projects.

Date	Lesson	Host Home	Dessert/Meal	Leader
Monday, January 15	1	Steve/Laura's	Joe	Bill

PERSONAL HEALTH PLAN

This worksheet could become your single most important feature in this study. On it you can record your personal priorities before the Father. It will help you live a healthy spiritual life, balancing all five of God's purposes.

PURPOSE	PLAN
CONNECT	WHO are you connecting with spiritually?
GROW	WHAT is your next step for growth?
DEVELOP	WHERE are you serving?
SHARE	WHEN are you shepherding another in Christ?
SURRENDER	HOW are you surrendering your heart?

DATE	MY PROGRESS	PARTNER'S PROGRESS

SAMPLE
PERSONAL HEALTH PLAN

This worksheet could become your single most important feature in this study. On it you can record your personal priorities before the Father. It will help you live a healthy spiritual life, balancing all five of God's purposes.

PURPOSE	PLAN
CONNECT	WHO are you connecting with spiritually? *Bill and I will meet weekly by email or phone*
GROW	WHAT is your next step for growth? *Regular devotions or journaling my prayers 2x/week*
DEVELOP	WHERE are you serving? *Serving in Children's Ministry* *Go through GIFTS Class*
SHARE	WHEN are you shepherding another in Christ? *Shepherding Bill at lunch or hosting a starter group in the fall*
SURRENDER	HOW are you surrendering your heart? *Help with our teenager* *New job situation*

DATE	MY PROGRESS	PARTNER'S PROGRESS
3/5	Talked during our group	Figured out our goals together
3/12	Missed our time together	Missed our time together
3/26	Met for coffee and review of my goals	Met for coffee
4/10	Emailed prayer requests	Bill sent me his prayer requests
3/5	Great start on personal journaling	Read Mark 1 – 6 in one sitting!
3/12	Traveled and not doing well this week	Journaled about Christ as Healer
3/26	Back on track	Busy and distracted; asked for prayer
3/1	Need to call Children's Pastor	
3/26	Group did a serving project together	Agreed to lead group worship
3/30	Regularly rotating leadership	Led group worship — great job!
3/5	Called Jim to see if he's open to joining our group	Wanted to invite somebody, but didn't
3/12	Preparing to start a group in fall	
3/30	Group prayed for me	Told friend something he's learning about Christ
3/5	Overwhelmed but encouraged	Scared to lead worship
3/15	Felt heard and more settled	Issue with wife
3/30	Read book on teens	Glad he took on his fear

PERSONAL HEALTH ASSESSMENT

	JUST BEGINNING	GETTING GOING	WELL DEVELOPED

CONNECTING WITH GOD AND OTHERS

I am deepening my understanding of and friendship
with God in community with others. — 1 2 3 4 5

I am growing in my ability both to share and to
show my love to others. — 1 2 3 4 5

I am willing to share my real needs for prayer and
support from others. — 1 2 3 4 5

I am resolving conflict constructively and am
willing to forgive others. — 1 2 3 4 5

CONNECTING TOTAL _____

GROWING IN YOUR SPIRITUAL JOURNEY

I have a growing relationship with God through regular
time in the Bible and in prayer (spiritual habits). — 1 2 3 4 5

I am experiencing more of the characteristics of
Jesus Christ (love, patience, gentleness, courage,
self-control, and so forth) in my life. — 1 2 3 4 5

I am avoiding addictive behaviors (food, television,
busyness, and the like) to meet my needs. — 1 2 3 4 5

I am spending time with a Christian friend (spiritual partner)
who celebrates and challenges my spiritual growth. — 1 2 3 4 5

GROWING TOTAL _____

SERVING WITH YOUR GOD-GIVEN DESIGN

I have discovered and am further developing my
unique God-given design. — 1 2 3 4 5

I am regularly praying for God to show me
opportunities to serve him and others. — 1 2 3 4 5

I am serving in a regular (once a month or more)
ministry in the church or community. — 1 2 3 4 5

I am a team player in my small group by sharing
some group role or responsibility. — 1 2 3 4 5

SERVING TOTAL _____

SHARING GOD'S LOVE IN EVERYDAY LIFE

I am cultivating relationships with non-Christians and praying
    for God to give me natural opportunities to share his love.   1 2 3 4 5

I am praying and learning about where God can use me
    and my group cross-culturally for missions.   1 2 3 4 5

I am investing my time in another person or group who
    needs to know Christ.   1 2 3 4 5

I am regularly inviting unchurched or unconnected
    friends to my church or small group.   1 2 3 4 5

SHARING TOTAL _____

SURRENDERING YOUR LIFE TO GOD

I am experiencing more of the presence and
    power of God in my everyday life.   1 2 3 4 5

I am faithfully attending services and my
    small group to worship God.   1 2 3 4 5

I am seeking to please God by surrendering every
    area of my life (health, decisions, finances,
    relationships, future, and the like) to him.   1 2 3 4 5

I am accepting the things I cannot change and
    becoming increasingly grateful for the life I've been given.   1 2 3 4 5

SURRENDERING TOTAL _____

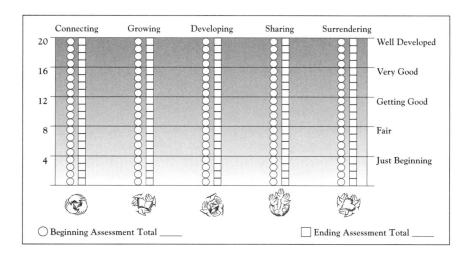

TEAM ROLES

The Bible makes clear that every group member, not just the leader, is a minister in the body of Christ. In a healthy small group, every member takes on some small role or responsibility. It's more fun and effective if you team up on these roles.

Review the team roles and responsibilities on the following pages, then have each member volunteer for a role or participate on a team. If someone doesn't know where to serve or is holding back, have the group suggest a team or role. It's best to have one or two people on each team so you have each of the five purposes covered. Serving in even a small capacity will not only help your leader but also will make the group more fun for everyone. Don't hold back. Join a team!

The opportunities are broken down by the five purposes and then by a "crawl" (beginning step), "walk" (intermediate step), or "run" (advanced step). Try to cover at least the crawl and walk roles, and select a role that matches your group, your gifts, and your maturity. If you can't find a good step or just want to see other ideas, go to www.lifetogether.com and see what other groups are choosing.

TEAM ROLES	TEAM PLAYER(S)

CONNECTING TEAM (Fellowship and Community Building)

		TEAM PLAYER(S)
Crawl:	Host a social event or group activity in the first week or two.	_____ _____
Walk:	Create a list of uncommitted members and then invite them to an open house or group social.	_____ _____
Run:	Plan a twenty-four-hour retreat or weekend getaway for the group. Lead the Connecting time each week for the group.	_____ _____

GROWING TEAM (Discipleship and Spiritual Growth)

Crawl: Coordinate the spiritual partners for the   _____
group. Facilitate a three- or four-person   _____
discussion circle during the Bible study
portion of your meeting. Coordinate the
discussion circles.

Walk: Tabulate the Personal Health Assessments   _____
and Health Plans in a summary to let   _____
people know how you're doing as a group.
Encourage personal devotions through group discussions
and pairing up with spiritual (accountability) partners.

Run: Take the group on a prayer walk, or plan   _____
a day of solitude, fasting, or personal retreat.   _____

SERVING TEAM (Discovering Your God-Given Design for Ministry)

Crawl: Ensure that every member finds a   _____
group role or team he or she enjoys.   _____

Walk: Have every member take a gift test   _____
(see www.lifetogether.com) and   _____
determine your group's gifts. Plan a
ministry project together.

Run: Help each member decide on a   _____
way to use his or her unique gifts   _____
somewhere in the church.

SHARING TEAM (SHARING AND EVANGELISM)

Crawl: Coordinate the group's Prayer and   _____
Praise Report of friends and family   _____
who don't know Christ.

Walk: Search for group mission opportunities   _____
and plan a cross-cultural group activity.   _____

Run: Take a small-group "vacation" to host a   _____
six-week group in your neighborhood   _____
or office. Then come back together
with your current group.

SURRENDERING TEAM (Surrendering Your Heart to Worship)

Crawl: Maintain the group's Prayer
         and Praise Report.   _____

                                             _____

Walk: Lead a brief time of worship each   _____
         week (at the beginning or end of
         your meeting), either a cappella or _____
         using a song from the DVD or the
         LIFE TOGETHER Worship DVD/CD.

Run: Plan a unique time of worship through _____
         Communion, foot washing, night of
         prayer, or nature walking.   _____

GIFTS INVENTORY

*A spiritual gift is given to each of us as a means of helping
the entire church. (1 Corinthians 12:7 NLT)*

A spiritual gift is a special ability given by the Holy Spirit to every believer at conversion. Although spiritual gifts are given when the Holy Spirit enters new believers, their use and purpose need to be understood and developed as we grow spiritually. A spiritual gift is much like a muscle: the more you use it, the stronger it becomes.

A FEW TRUTHS ABOUT SPIRITUAL GIFTS

- Only believers have spiritual gifts. (1 Corinthians 2:14)
- You can't earn or work for a spiritual gift. (Ephesians 4:7)
- The Holy Spirit decides what gifts I get. (1 Corinthians 12:11)
- I am to develop the gifts God gives me. (Romans 11:29; 2 Timothy 1:6)
- It's a sin to waste the gifts God gave me. (1 Corinthians 4:1 – 2; Matthew 25:14 – 30)
- Using my gifts honors God and expands me. (John 15:8)

GIFTS INVENTORY

God wants us to know what spiritual gift(s) he has given us. One person can have many gifts. The goal is to find the areas in which the Holy Spirit seems to have supernaturally empowered our service to others. These gifts are to be used to minister to others and build up the body of Christ.

There are four main lists of gifts found in the Bible: Romans 12:3 – 8; 1 Corinthians 12:1 – 11, 27 – 31; Ephesians 4:11 – 12; and 1 Peter 4:9 – 11. There are other passages that mention or illustrate gifts not included in these lists. As you read through the following list, prayerfully consider whether the biblical definition describes you. Remember, you can have more than one gift, but everyone has at least one.

ADMINISTRATION (Organization)—1 Corinthians 12

This is the ability to recognize the gifts of others and recruit them to a ministry. It is the ability to organize and manage people, resources, and time for effective ministry.

APOSTLE—1 Corinthians 12

This is the ability to start new churches/ventures and oversee their development.

DISCERNMENT—1 Corinthians 12

This is the ability to distinguish between the spirit of truth and the spirit of error; to detect inconsistencies in another's life and confront in love.

ENCOURAGEMENT (Exhortation)—Romans 12

This is the ability to motivate God's people to apply and act on biblical principles, especially when they are discouraged or wavering in their faith. It is also the ability to bring out the best in others and challenge them to develop their potential.

EVANGELISM—Ephesians 4

This is the ability to communicate the gospel of Jesus Christ to unbelievers in a positive, nonthreatening way and to sense opportunities to share Christ and lead people to respond with faith.

FAITH—1 Corinthians 12

This is the ability to trust God for what cannot be seen and to act on God's promise, regardless of what the circumstances indicate. This includes a willingness to risk failure in pursuit of a God-given vision, expecting God to handle the obstacles.

GIVING—Romans 12

This is the ability to generously contribute material resources and/or money beyond the 10 percent tithe so that the church may grow and be strengthened. It includes the ability to manage money so it may be given to support the ministry of others.

HOSPITALITY — 1 Peter 4:9–10

This is the ability to make others, especially strangers, feel warmly welcomed, accepted, and comfortable in the church family; also the ability to coordinate factors that promote fellowship.

LEADERSHIP — Romans 12

This is the ability to clarify and communicate the purpose and direction ("vision") of a ministry in a way that attracts others to get involved; it includes the ability to motivate others, by example, to work together in accomplishing a ministry goal.

MERCY — Romans 12

This is the ability to manifest practical, compassionate, cheerful love toward suffering members of the body of Christ.

PASTORING (Shepherding) — Ephesians 4

This is the ability to care for the spiritual needs of a group of believers and equip them for ministry. It is also the ability to nurture a small group in spiritual growth and assume responsibility for their welfare.

PREACHING — Romans 12

This is the ability to publicly communicate God's Word in an inspired way that convinces unbelievers and both challenges and comforts believers.

SERVICE — Romans 12

This is the ability to recognize unmet needs in the church family and to take the initiative to provide practical assistance quickly, cheerfully, and without need for recognition.

TEACHING — Ephesians 4

This is the ability to educate God's people by clearly explaining and applying the Bible in a way that causes them to learn; it is the ability to equip and train other believers for ministry.

WISDOM — 1 Corinthians 12

This is the ability to understand God's perspective on life situations and share those insights in a simple, understandable way.

PERFORMING A FOOTWASHING

In John 13:1–17 Jesus makes it quite clear to his disciples that his position as the Father's Son includes being a servant, not just the divine privileges of power and glory. To properly understand the scene and Jesus' intention, we must realize that footwashing was the duty of slaves and indeed of non-Jewish rather than Jewish slaves. Yet Jesus placed himself in the position of a servant. He displayed to the disciples self-sacrifice and love ("that you also should do what I have done to you"—John 13:15). In view of his majesty, only the symbolic position of a slave was adequate to open their eyes and keep them from lofty illusions.

The point of footwashing, then, is to correct the attitude that Jesus discerned in the disciples. It constitutes the permanent basis for mutual service, service in your group and for the community around you, which is laid on all Christians.

WHEN TO IMPLEMENT

Under "How to Prepare" for a footwashing, we'll talk about the importance of earning the right to do a footwashing. When to implement a footwashing in your "group time" can be as important as "earning the right." There are three primary places we would recommend you insert a footwashing: (1) during a break in the Surrendering section of your group; (2) during a break in the Growing section of your group; or (3) at the closing of your group. A special time of prayer for each person as their feet are washed can be added to the footwashing time.

HOW TO PREPARE

What you need:

- Towels: For the washing and drying of each set of feet.
- Bowls: Make sure you have enough bowls to be able to have fresh water for washing and rinsing.
- Liquid soap: Not a necessity, but a nice touch.

Things to be considerate of:

- The opposite sex: Men wash men's feet, women wash women's feet.
- Religious upbringing: Be sensitive to where your group is coming from.
- Know your group: Be sensitive to the bonding of your group.
- Earn the right: Make sure you have enough meetings under your belt for your group to know your heart and get the full impact of the footwashing.
- Know your options: If someone in your group has limitations (i.e., a lady may come wearing stockings, a person may have an open wound or cast) or is uncomfortable with the washing of feet, see if you can wash the hands, see if the spouse (if there is one) can wash the feet, and give the person the right to "pass."

Attitude and objectives:

- Be in an attitude of prayer for what God can do in and through you. Communicate servanthood.
- Understand the attitude of humility (both on the "giving" and "receiving" end).
- Pray for the best time to do a footwashing in your group. Timing is everything.

Some neat ideas:

- After the footwashing, you may want to give each member of your group a new pair of socks to put on to enjoy the rest of the group time.
- Before sending a member of the group on a mission trip or to multiply a new group, do a footwashing to serve them before they go out to serve.

LEADING
FOR THE FIRST TIME

- **Sweaty palms are a healthy sign.** The Bible says God is gracious to the humble. Remember who is in control; the time to worry is when you're not worried. Those who are soft in heart (and sweaty palmed) are those whom God is sure to speak through.
- **Seek support.** Ask your leader, coleader, or close friend to pray for you and prepare with you before the session. Walking through the study will help you anticipate potentially difficult questions and discussion topics.
- **Bring your uniqueness to the study.** Lean into who you are and how God wants you to uniquely lead the study.
- **Prepare. Prepare. Prepare.** Read the Introduction and Leader's Notes for the session you are leading. Consider writing in a journal or fasting for a day to prepare yourself for what God wants to do.
- **Don't wait until the last minute to prepare.**
- **Ask for feedback so you can grow.** Perhaps in an email or on cards handed out at the study, have everyone write down three things you did well and one thing you could improve on. Don't get defensive, but show an openness to learn and grow.
- **Prayerfully consider launching a new group.** This doesn't need to happen overnight, but God's heart is for this to happen over time. Not all Christians are called to be leaders or teachers, but we are all called to be "shepherds" of a few someday.
- **Share with your group what God is doing in your heart.** God is searching for those whose hearts are fully his. Share your trials and victories. We promise that people will relate.

INTRODUCTION

Congratulations! You have responded to the call to help shepherd Jesus' flock. There are few other tasks in the family of God that surpass the contribution you will be making. As you prepare to lead this small group, there are a few thoughts to keep in mind:

Review the "Read Me First" on pages 9–11 so you'll understand the purpose of each section in the study. If this is your first time leading a small group, turn to Leading for the First Time section on page 106 of the appendix for suggestions.

Remember that you are not alone. God knows everything about you, and he knew that you would be leading this group. God promises, "Never will I leave you; never will I forsake you" (Hebrews 13:5b).

Your role as leader. Create a safe, warm environment for your group. As a leader, your most important job is to create an atmosphere where people are willing to talk honestly about what the topics discussed in this study have to do with them. Be available before people arrive so you can greet them at the door. People are naturally nervous at a new group, so a hug or handshake can help put them at ease.

Prepare for each meeting ahead of time. Review the Leader's Notes and write down your responses to each study question. Pay special attention to exercises that ask group members to do something other than engage in discussion. These exercises will help your group live what the Bible teaches, not just talk about it. Be sure you understand how an exercise works, and bring any necessary supplies (such a paper or pens) to your meeting.

Pray for your group members by name. Before you begin each session, go around the room in your mind and pray for each member by name. You may want to review the prayer list at least once a week. Ask God to use your time together to touch the heart of every person uniquely. Expect God to lead you to those he wants you to encourage or challenge in a special way.

Discuss expectations. Ask everyone to tell what he or she hopes to get out of this study. You might want to review the Small Group Agreement (see pages 89–90) and talk about each person's expectations and priorities. You could discuss whether you want to do the For Deeper Study for homework before each meeting. Review the Small Group Calendar on page 91 and talk about who else is willing to open their home to host or facilitate a meeting.

Don't try to go it alone. Pray for God to help you, and enlist help from the members of your group. You will find your experience to be richer and more rewarding if you enable group members to help — and you'll be able to help group members discover their individual gifts for serving or even leading the group.

Plan a kick-off meeting. We recommend that you plan a kick-off meeting where you will pray, hand out study guides, spend some time getting to know each other, and discuss each person's expectations for the group. A meeting like this is a great way to start a group or step up people's commitments.

A simple meal, potluck, or even good desserts make a kick-off meeting more fun. After dessert, have everyone respond to an icebreaker question, such as, "How did you hear of our church, and what's one thing you love about it?" Or, "Tell us three things about your life growing up that most people here don't know."

If you aren't able to hold a "get to know you" meeting before you launch into session one, consider starting the first meeting half an hour early to give people time to socialize without shortchanging your time in the study. For example, you can have social time from 7:00 to 7:30, and by 7:40 you'll gather the group with a prayer. Even if only a few people are seated in the living room by 7:40, ask them to join you in praying for those who are coming and for God to be present among you as you meet. Others will notice you praying and will come and sit down. You may want to softly play music from a LIFE TOGETHER Worship CD or other worship CD as people arrive and then turn up the volume when you are ready to begin. This first night will set the tone for the whole six weeks.

You may ask a few people to come early to help set up, pray, and introduce newcomers to others. Even if everyone is new, they don't know that yet and may be shy when they arrive. You might give people roles like setting up name tags or handing out drinks. This could be a great way to spot a coleader.

Subgrouping. If your group has more than seven people, break into discussion groups of two to four people for the Growing and Surrendering sections each week. People will connect more with the study and each other when they have more opportunity to participate. Smaller discussion circles encourage quieter people to talk more and tend to minimize the effects of more vocal or dominant members. Also, people who are unaccustomed to praying aloud will feel more comfortable praying within a smaller group of people. Consider sharing prayer requests in the larger group and then break into smaller groups to pray for each other. People are more willing to pray in small circles if they know that the whole group will hear all the prayer requests.

Memorizing Scripture. Although we have not provided specific verses for the group to memorize, this is something you can encourage the group to do each week. One benefit of memorizing God's Word is noted by the psalmist in Psalm 119:11: "I have hidden your word in my heart that I might not sin against you."

Anyone who has memorized Scripture can confirm the amazing spiritual benefits that result from this practice. Don't miss out on the opportunity to encourage your group to grow in the knowledge of God's Word through Scripture memorization.

Reflections. We've provided opportunity for a personal time with God using the Reflections at the end of each session. Don't press seekers to do this, but just remind the group that every believer should have a plan for personal time with God.

Invite new people. Finally, cast the vision, as Jesus did, to be inclusive not exclusive. Ask everyone to prayerfully think of people who would enjoy or benefit from a group like this. The beginning of a new study is a great time to welcome a few people into your circle. Have each person share a name or two and either make phone calls the coming week or handwrite invitations or postcards that very night. This will make it fun and also make it happen. Don't worry about ending up with too many people — you can always have one discussion circle in the living room and another in the dining room.

SESSION 1:
INFLUENTIAL SERVICE — MOSES

As leader, your most important job is to create an atmosphere where people are willing to talk honestly about what the topics discussed in this study have to do with them. If your group is new and you aren't able to hold a kick-off meeting before you launch into session one, consider starting your first meeting half an hour early to give people time to socialize without short-changing your time in the study. For example, you can have social time from 7:00 to 7:30, and by 7:40 you'll gather the group with a prayer. Even if only a few people are seated in the living room by 7:40, ask them to join you in prayer for those who are coming and for God to be present among you as you meet. Others will notice you praying and will come and sit down. You may want to softly play music from a LIFE TOGETHER Worship DVD/CD (you can find them at www.lifetogether.com) or other worship CD as people arrive, and turn up the volume when you are ready to begin. This first night will set the tone for the whole six weeks.

You may want to ask a few people to come early to help set up, pray, and introduce newcomers to others. Even if everyone is new, they don't know that yet and may be shy when they arrive. You might give people roles like setting up name tags or handing out drinks. This could be a great way to spot a coleader.

CONNECTING. Question 1. We've designed this study for both new and established groups. New groups need to invest more time in building relationships with each other, while established groups often want to dig deeper into Bible study and application. Begin your group time with this icebreaker question to get people relaxed and focused on the session topic. You should be the first to answer this question while others are thinking about how to respond. Be sure to give everyone a chance to answer, because it's a chance for the group to get to know each other. It's not necessary to go around the circle in order. Just ask for volunteers to respond.

Introduction to the Series. Take a moment after question 1 to orient the group to one principle that undergirds this series: A healthy small group balances the purposes of the church. Most small groups emphasize Bible study, fellowship, and prayer. But God has called us to reach out to others as well.

He wants us to *do* what Jesus teaches, not just *learn* about it. You may spend less time in this series studying the Bible than some group members are used to. That's because you'll spend more time *doing* things the Bible says believers should do.

However, those who like more Bible study can find plenty of it in this series. For Deeper Study provides additional passages you can dig into for each session topic. If your group likes to do deeper Bible study, consider having members answer next week's Growing section questions ahead of time as homework. They can even study next week's For Deeper Study passages for homework too. Then, during the Growing portion of your meeting, you can share the high points of what you've learned.

If the five biblical purposes are new to your group, be sure to review them together on pages 9–10 of the Read Me First section.

Question 2. As leader, you're in the people development business. Part of your job is to help others discover and develop their gifts. You may not need their help to host or lead a meeting, but they need you to let them take on a role and support them so that they succeed. If you have children, you know that it's often easier to do a job yourself than to help one of them learn to do it. But that's what Jesus did with his disciples, and it's what he wants us to do for those we lead.

Question 3. A Small Group Agreement helps you clarify your group's priorities and cast new vision for what the group can be. Members can imagine what your group could be like if they lived these values. So turn to pages 89–90 and choose one or two values that you want to emphasize in this study. We also suggest reviewing the Frequently Asked Questions on pages 86–88 to gain an understanding of how the group should function and answer any questions that may come up.

GROWING. Each Growing section begins with an opening story and a passage of Scripture. Have someone read the opening story and someone else read the Bible passage aloud. It's a good idea to ask someone ahead of time, because not everyone is comfortable reading aloud in public. When the passage has been read, ask the questions that follow. It is not necessary that everyone answer every question in the Bible study. In fact, a group can become boring if you simply go around the circle and give answers. Your goal is to create a discussion—which means that perhaps only a few people respond to each question and an engaging dialogue gets going. It's even fine to skip some questions in order to spend more time on questions you believe are most important.

Remember to use the Study Notes as you go through this section to add depth and understanding to your study.

Questions 4–12. Moses knew he couldn't do what God was asking on his own power. Encourage group discussion about (1) the reasons for Moses' response, and (2) God's part in the eventual outcome. Was Moses reluctant or modest? Yes, he felt ill-equipped and inadequate, but how many of our fleshly decisions are influenced by our own opinions of our abilities? God will be with us and give us what we need when he calls us to a task.

DEVELOPING. Question 14. For those who haven't done a LIFE TOGETHER study before, "spiritual partners" will be a new idea. This addresses the practice of having an accountability partner, someone who will commit to pray and hold you accountable for spiritual goals and progress. This may be the single most important habit your group members can take away from this study. Encourage everyone to partner with one other person, two at the most. In this session we encourage you to become familiar with and begin to use the Personal Health Plan to challenge and track your spiritual goals and progress as well as your partner's. There is one Personal Health Plan in the appendix, so be sure to have a few extra copies on hand at your first meeting for groups of three spiritual partners.

SHARING. Question 15. God calls all believers to share the good news about Jesus with those who don't know him. Challenge the group to make the most of this opportunity to reach out to a seeker or someone who isn't even sure that God exists. Have them write at least one person's name in the space provided. Encourage group members to pray for an opportunity to get to know these individuals more, invite them to the group, or share a part of their own story with them. Encourage your group to do their part and trust God to touch the hearts of those they have listed.

Question 16. Take this opportunity to get an up-to-date Small Group Roster started during this time.

SURRENDERING. Question 17. One of the most important aspects of every small group meeting is the prayer support we offer to one another. The Surrendering section gives you the opportunity to share needs and know that the group will be faithful to pray. As leader, you want to be sure to allow time for this important part of small group life.

Never pressure a person to pray aloud. That's a sure way to scare someone away from your group. Instead of praying in a circle (which makes it obvious when someone stays silent), allow open time when anyone can pray who wishes to do so. Have someone write down everyone's prayer requests on the

Prayer and Praise Report on page 22. If your time is short, consider having people share requests and pray just with their spiritual partners or in smaller circles of two to four.

Question 18. Here is your opportunity to encourage your group to embrace Scripture reading and time with God by using the Reflections throughout the week. Remind them of how regular time with God and his Word will reap the reward of spiritual growth for those willing to give themselves to it. Maybe you or someone else in the group can share a personal story of the impact this important habit has made.

As you begin, welcome any new people and praise the ones who brought them. Renew the vision to welcome people for one more week and model this if you can. Then have everyone sit back, relax, close their eyes, and listen to one of the songs on a Life Together Worship CD, or other worship CD. You may want to sing the second time through as a group, or simply take a few moments of silence to focus on God and transition from the distractions of your day.

CONNECT. Question 1. Begin your group time with this icebreaker question to get people relaxed and focused on the session topic. You should be the first to answer this question while others are thinking about how to respond. Be sure to give everyone a chance to respond, because it's a chance for the group to get to know each other. It's not necessary to go around the circle in order. Just ask for volunteers to respond.

Question 2. In this session, encourage the group to evaluate their spiritual health using the Personal Health Assessment on pages 96–97 of the appendix. Familiarize yourself with the Personal Health Assessment before the meeting. You may want to take the assessment yourself ahead of time and think about your goal. Then you can give group members a real-life example of what you are actually committed to doing. Encourage each group member to take the time to write in a simple step (or goal) under the "WHAT is your next step for growth?" question on the Personal Health Plan on page 92 and encourage accountability for taking the step this week.

Question 3. Checking in with your spiritual partners will be an option in all sessions from now on. As leader, we encourage you to complete a simple goal under each purpose to share with your group. Ask your coleader or a trusted friend to review it with you. Then you'll understand the power of this tool and the support you can gain from a spiritual partner. During this time, encourage group members to pair up with their spiritual partner and discuss question 3.

If newcomers have joined you, take a few minutes before the Growing section to let all members introduce themselves. You could even let each member share one thing he or she has liked about the group so far, and let the newcomers tell who invited them. The first visit to a new group is scary, so be sure to minimize the inside jokes. Introduce newcomers to some highly relational people when they arrive and partner them with great spiritual partners to welcome them at their first meeting.

We highly recommend that, as leader, you read the Study Notes ahead of time and draw the group's attention to anything there that will help them better understand the Bible passage and how it applies to their lives.

GROWING. Questions 4 – 9. Stepping out for God requires trust. Have someone read the Scripture or take turns reading, and then lead the group through the discussion questions that follow. Consider that when we yield to God's will, great things happen. People notice. What's important is that God prepares us, then uses us and the abilities he gives us. Our success belongs to God and he rewards us for our obedience.

DEVELOPING. Question 10. People need to go beyond theorizing about service to actually doing it. Try to come to this question prepared to get the discussion started with your own personal examples and ideas.

Question 11. This exercise is designed to help group members identify their individual gifts and then discuss what roles they can take within the group based on what they learn. We recommend that you, as leader, familiarize yourself with the Gifts Inventory on pages 101 – 103 of the appendix ahead of time. Also, evaluate the Team Roles on pages 98 – 100 to see ways that the group's talents can be used in God's service.

SHARING. Question 12. Take time here to plan a service outreach for the group. Ask for a volunteer (or appoint one if no one responds) to research ideas and report back to the group in session five.

SURRENDERING. Question 13. Let the group share their prayer requests and be sure to use the Prayer and Praise Report to record the requests. Having the prayer requests written down will prompt you to pray for each member, as well as remind you of God's faithfulness as your group sees answers. After requests have been recorded, spend some time praying together for them.

Question 14. We've provided opportunity for a personal time with God throughout the week using the Reflections at the end of each session. Don't press seekers to do this, but every believer should have a plan for personal time with God.

SESSION 3: COMMUNITY-BUILDING SERVICE — NEHEMIAH

In order to maximize your time together and honor the diversity of personality types, do your best to begin and end your group on time. Remember, if you wait for people to arrive before starting, you are training them to know they aren't really late. If your group meets on weeknights when people need to get up early the next morning, it is unfair to begin and end later than you agreed upon. You may even want to adjust your starting or stopping time if it seems necessary. Don't hesitate to open in prayer even before everyone is seated. This isn't disrespectful of those who are still gathering — it respects those who are ready to begin, and the others won't be offended. An opening prayer can be as simple as "Welcome, Lord! Help us! Now let's start."

If you've had trouble getting through all of the Bible study questions, consider breaking into smaller circles of four or five people for the Bible study (Growing) portion of your meeting. Everyone will get more "airtime," and the people who tend to dominate the discussion will be balanced out. A circle of four doesn't need an experienced leader, and it's a great way to identify and train a coleader. Also remember that if people are silent before they answer a question, it's because they're thinking!

CONNECTING. Questions 1 – 2. Choose whichever icebreaker best fits your group. You should be the first to answer this question while others are thinking about how to respond. Be sure to give everyone a chance to respond to this question, because it's a chance for the group to get to know each other. It's not necessary to go around the circle in order. Just ask for volunteers.

Question 3. Check in with spiritual partners. You'll need to watch the clock and keep these conversations to ten minutes. If partners want more time together (as is ideal), they can connect before, after, or outside meetings. Give them a two-minute notice and hold to it if you ever want to get them back in the circle! If some group members are absent or newcomers have joined you, you may need to connect people with new or temporary partners.

If you prefer (and especially if there are many newcomers), you can choose to use the lighter icebreaker question for the whole group. We encourage you, though, to let partners check in during group time at least every other week so that those relationships grow solid. Please don't miss this opportunity to take your people deeper. Remember that the goal here is "transforming lives through community," and one-on-one time has an enormous return on time spent. In a week or two, you might want to ask the group how their partnerships are going. This will encourage those who are struggling to connect or accomplish their goals.

GROWING. For the Growing section, be sure to familiarize yourself with the Study Notes so you can help the group better understand Nehemiah's situation.

Someone read the Scripture or take turns reading. Then discuss these questions in light of the Scripture reading.

Questions 7 – 10. The purpose of the exercise in question 7 is to get people to recognize the needs around them and how they can motivate others into action to resolve them. You might want to answer these questions yourself in advance of the meeting so you are able to get the discussion started.

DEVELOPING. Questions 11 – 13. Use these questions to guide the group to an understanding of how they can begin to use their abilities to serve the group and the body of Christ.

Question 14. Take a few minutes during this session to plan a group social — a time when you can all get together in an informal setting to share a meal or fun activity. Encourage everyone to use their individual talents to make this a special event for your group. This could be a dinner out, a potluck, a night of bowling or going to a movie — whatever you want. Ask for volunteers to plan this event and report ideas to the group in session five.

If you think you might not get volunteers easily, you may want to take people aside before the meeting starts and ask them to consider taking on a role. Let people say no if they choose.

SHARING. Question 15. How can your group meet specific needs within your community or the nation? Come to the meeting prepared to share some ideas to get the conversation rolling.

Question 16. The Circles of Life represent one of the values of the Small Group Agreement: "Welcome for Newcomers." Some groups fear that newcomers will interrupt the intimacy that members have built over time. However, groups generally gain strength with the infusion of new blood. It's like a river of living water flowing into a stagnant pond.

Some groups remain permanently open, while others open periodically, such as at the beginning and end of a study. Love grows by giving itself away. If your circle becomes too large for easy, face-to-face conversations, you can simply form a second discussion circle in another room of your home.

As leader, you should do this exercise yourself in advance and be ready to share the names of the people you're going to invite or connect with. Your modeling is the number-one example that people will follow. Give everyone a few moments to write down names before each person shares. You might pray for a few of these names on the spot and/or later in the session. Encourage people not to be afraid to ask someone. Almost no one is annoyed to be invited to something! Most people are honored to be asked, even if they can't make it. You may want to hand out invitations and fill them out during the meeting.

SURRENDERING. Question 17. Be sure to save time to pray for each other. In this session we encourage you to break into small groups of two or three for prayer.

There are bound to be people in your group who long for healing, whether physical or emotional, and this will come out during prayer request time. Some churches emphasize prayer for healing—if yours does, follow your church's practice in the way you approach this. Other churches prefer to avoid a charismatic flavor in their small groups—if yours has that concern, pray for one another in whatever way seems comfortable. If you're concerned that some members might confuse or try to "fix" others through prayer, pray as a whole group and monitor how people pray. But don't be overly concerned: the very worst that will happen is that someone will pray in a way that distresses someone else, and if that happens you can simply talk to each person privately before your next meeting. As leader, you set the example of how people will pray for each other in your group, and most members will follow your lead.

Question 18. Continue to encourage your group to take the opportunity for a personal time with God throughout the week using the Reflections at the end of each session.

SESSION 4:
OBEDIENT SERVICE — NOAH

The Bible is clear that every Christian is meant to be a servant of Christ. We strongly recommend that you challenge your members to take whatever step to which they sense God is calling them. You will need to model here. Don't miss the need people have to grow through sharing responsibilities to host the group.

CONNECTING. Questions 1–2. Choose whichever icebreaker best fits your group. You should be the first to answer this question while others are thinking about how to respond. Be sure to give everyone a chance to respond to this question, because it's a chance for the group to get to know each other. It's not necessary to go around the circle in order. Just ask for volunteers.

Question 3. As you encourage your group members to check in with their spiritual partners this week, you might want to ask them to share how their partnerships are going. This will encourage those who are struggling to connect or accomplish their goals.

GROWING. Questions 4–9. Have someone read the Scripture aloud to the group. God gave Noah very detailed instructions of what to do. And though Noah had never done anything like this before in his life, his heart was prepared for the task. How? Examine what your group's response would be to a similar assignment.

DEVELOPING. Questions 10–11. Service should always be an expression of love. Among the people of God, no one should be forced to serve or be manipulated into serving. Those who serve because they fear those they serve, or because of guilt or manipulation, need the church's support in addressing those situations. The most loving thing the community can do for those who demand service, or who manipulate others, is to confront them about this behavior. Jesus was fearless and not subject to manipulation, so he could serve out of love. Encourage the group to explore their lives to discover what their God-given talents might be, and then discuss question 11.

Question 12. In this session we want you to be thinking about this group continuing to meet for another study and, if so, what you might study next.

SHARING. Questions 13–14. Think ahead of time about how you would answer these questions and be ready to kick off the discussion.

SURRENDERING. Question 15. Have the group share their prayer requests and be sure to use the Prayer and Praise Report to record them. Having the prayer requests written down will prompt you to pray for each member, as well as remind you of God's faithfulness as your group sees answers. After requests have been recorded, spend some time praying as a group. Encourage group members to continue to pray for each other between meetings.

Question 16. Make sure everyone understands what footwashing signified in ancient culture. It's important to strip the glamor off servanthood. Serving can be dirty and thankless, like caring for small children with messy diapers. Jesus had no self-focused motives for serving. He did it because he loved his disciples and wanted them to learn to love each other in the same way.

If you really want to bring home this message to your group, wash some people's feet as they arrive or during the meeting. If you're worried about people saying no, wash your spouse's or coleader's feet. This will create a memory that you and your group will never forget. One group did this and still describes the evening as one of the most memorable in their group's ten-year history. Have a chair, warm water, soft music, and a stack of towels ready.

Question 17. Continue to encourage group members to use the Reflections verses at the end of each session for personal time with God. Don't press seekers to do this, but every believer should have a plan for personal time with God.

SESSION 5:
TIMELY SERVICE — ESTHER

Remember, in order to maximize your time together and honor your group, do your best to begin and end your group on time. Announce the opening prayer, even before everyone is seated, to indicate that you are ready to begin.

CONNECTING. Questions 1 – 2. Choose whichever icebreaker best fits your group. You should be the first to answer this question while others are thinking about how to respond. Be sure to give everyone a chance to respond to this question, because it's a chance for the group to get to know each other. It's not necessary to go around the circle in order. Just ask for volunteers.

Question 3. Start out by having your members check in with their spiritual partner(s), and assess how they are doing with their Health Plans and the goals they have set for themselves.

Question 4. In session three we suggested you get started on planning a party for your group. We suggest you have this event sometime the week after the last session of this study. Take some time here to discuss how your event is coming together. Has someone taken the lead for getting the party planned? Do you have all the volunteers you need to pull it off? If not, take some time to do this now.

GROWING. Questions 5 – 13. Encourage discussion on recognizing our opportunities to make a difference and acting on them.

DEVELOPING. Questions 14 – 16. To be available for God's work, we must understand what our priorities are and set them appropriately. Our thought life and how we spend our time and money are very good indicators of what is most important to us. The sad reality is that too frequently what we *say* we believe is important to us just doesn't match up with the evidence. How do you think this might affect our ability to see God's will for our lives? Self-examination is a valuable step toward accomplishing this, and it often reveals things we don't expect to find. Prayerfully work through the following exercises in advance of the meeting so that you will be able to lead the group through them and answer any questions they may have. Encourage the group members to share one area in which they need to see some changes. Ask the group to let their spiritual partner hold them accountable for their next step of growth.

SHARING. Question 18. In session two we suggested you get started on planning a service outreach for your group. We suggest you have this outreach as soon as is possible after the last session of this study. Take some time here to discuss how your plan is coming together. Ask the volunteer who was researching ideas to share those with the group now. Do you have all the volunteers you need to be effective? If not, take some time to do this now.

SURRENDERING. Question 19. Pray. Share prayer requests and record them in the Prayer and Praise Report.

Question 20. Continue to encourage group members to use the Reflections verses at the end of each session for personal time with God.

SESSION 6:
GIANT SERVICE—DAVID

You made it! This is the last session of this study! It's a time to celebrate where you've been and look forward to what's next for each of you and your group. If this is your first time leading the study, congratulations. Your goal for this meeting is to finish strong. It's also a time to think about God's final, ultimate purpose for you: surrendering your whole lives to him in worship, to give him pleasure.

CONNECTING. Questions 1–2. Choose whichever icebreaker best fits your group. You should be the first to answer this question while others are thinking about how to respond. Be sure to give everyone a chance to respond to this question, because it's a chance for the group to get to know each other. It's not necessary to go around the circle in order. Just ask for volunteers.

Question 3. Be sure to have spiritual partners check in with each other at this last meeting. Encourage them to review their Health Plans together to assess where they have grown and where they would still like to grow.

GROWING. Questions 4–9. Encourage the group to spend some time discovering what God has to say to them in the Scripture this week. Regardless of your experience, God can, and will, use you if you let him. God uniquely equipped David for the meeting with Goliath and he has uniquely equipped each group member for his appointments in their lives. Lead the group into being open to seeing all life's appointments from God's viewpoint and perspective.

DEVELOPING. Questions 10–11. Remember that your group may become boring if you let every group member answer every question. Two or three responses are plenty. Also remember that if people are silent before they answer, it's because they're thinking!

Question 12. Spend some time in this last meeting preparing your group to move forward. If your group is staying together, hopefully you've chosen your next study; if so, be sure to take the study guides to the meeting. Suggest that the group take another look at your Small Group Agreement to see if you want to change anything for the next study. Are all the values working for you, or is there some way your group could be improved by changing your expectations or living up to one of these values better than you have been?

You can make people feel safe talking about things they want to improve by first asking them what they've liked about the group. Set a positive tone. Then make sure people get to disagree respectfully, that everyone understands that they're speaking in confidence and won't be talked about outside the group, and that the goal of any changes will be the spiritual health of everyone.

SHARING. Question 13. Encourage group discussion regarding what they have learned from the story of David during this session.

SURRENDERING. Question 14. Plan to close your final session of this study with a footwashing. Instructions can be found on pages 104–105 of the appendix. Don't miss the opportunity to experience true humility in your group through this exercise. Plan to have everything ready to go at the start of the group meeting so that you don't have to spend group time in preparation.

Question 15. Whether your group is ending or continuing, it's important to celebrate where you have come together. Thank everyone for what they've contributed to the group. You might even give some thought ahead of time to something unique each person has contributed. Share your prayer requests and pray for each other before you close your meeting.

SMALL GROUP ROSTER

Name	Address	Phone	Email Address	Team or Role	Church Ministry
Bill Jones	7 Alvalar Street L.F. 92665	766-2255	bjones@aol.com	socials	children's ministry

(Pass your book around your group at your first meeting to get everyone's name and contact information.)

Name	Address	Phone	Email Address	Team or Role	Church Ministry

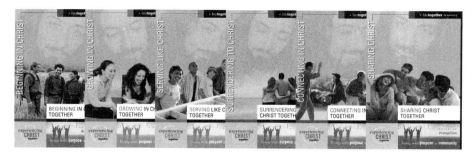

Experiencing Christ Together:

Living with Purpose in Community

Brett & Dee Eastman; Todd & Denise Wendorff; Karen Lee-Thorp

Experiencing Christ Together: Living with Purpose in Community is a series of six, six-week study guides that offers small groups a chance to explore Jesus' teaching on the five biblical purposes of the church. By closely examining Christ's life and teaching in the Gospels, the series helps group members walk in the steps of Christ's early followers. Jesus lived every moment following God's purposes for his life, and Experiencing Christ Together helps groups learn how they can do this too. The first book lays the foundation: who Christ is and what he has done for us. Each of the other five books in the series looks at how Jesus trained his followers to live one of the five biblical purposes (fellowship, discipleship, service, evangelism, and worship).

	Softcovers	DVD
Beginning in Christ Together	ISBN: 0-310-24986-4	ISBN: 0-310-26187-2
Connecting in Christ Together	ISBN: 0-310-24981-3	ISBN: 0-310-26189-9
Growing in Christ Together	ISBN: 0-310-24985-6	ISBN: 0-310-26192-9
Serving Like Christ Together	ISBN: 0-310-24984-8	ISBN: 0-310-26194-5
Sharing Christ Together	ISBN: 0-310-24983-X	ISBN: 0-310-26196-1
Surrendering to Christ Together	ISBN: 0-310-24982-1	ISBN: 0-310-26198-8

Pick up a copy today at your favorite bookstore!

Doing Life Together series

Brett & Dee Eastman; Todd & Denise Wendorff;
Karen Lee-Thorp

Based on the five biblical purposes that form the bedrock of Saddleback Church, Doing Life Together will help your group discover what God created you for and how you can turn this dream into an everyday reality. Experience the transformation firsthand as you begin Connecting, Growing, Developing, Sharing, and Surrendering your life together for him.

"Doing Life Together is a groundbreaking study . . . [It's] the first small group curriculum built completely on the purpose-driven paradigm . . . The greatest reason I'm excited about [it] is that I've seen the dramatic changes it produces in the lives of those who study it."

—From the foreword by Rick Warren

Small Group Ministry Consultation

Building a healthy, vibrant, and growing small group ministry is challenging. That's why Brett Eastman and a team of certified coaches are offering small group ministry consultation. Join pastors and church leaders from around the country to discover new ways to launch and lead a healthy Purpose-Driven small group ministry in your church. To find out more information please call 1-800-467-1977.

Softcover

Beginning Life Together	ISBN: 0-310-24672-5	ISBN: 0-310-25004-8
Connecting with God's Family	ISBN: 0-310-24673-3	ISBN: 0-310-25005-6
Growing to Be Like Christ	ISBN: 0-310-24674-1	ISBN: 0-310-25006-4
Developing Your SHAPE to Serve Others	ISBN: 0-310-24675-X	ISBN: 0-310-25007-2
Sharing Your Life Mission Every Day	ISBN: 0-310-24676-8	ISBN: 0-310-25008-0
Surrendering Your Life for God's Pleasure	ISBN: 0-310-24677-6	ISBN: 0-310-25009-9
Curriculum Kit	ISBN: 0-310-25002-1